THE SUBLIME LIFE OF MONASTICISM

THE SUBLIME LIFE OF MONASTICISM

by

His Grace Bishop Mettaous

ST SHENOUDA'S MONASTERY
SYDNEY, AUSTRALIA
2005

THE SUBLIME LIFE OF MONASTICISM

COPYRIGHT © 2005
St. Shenouda Coptic Orthodox Monastery

All rights reserved. Except for brief quotations in critical publications or reviews, no part of this book may be reproduced in any manner without prior written permission from the publisher.

ST SHENOUDA MONASTERY
8419 Putty Rd,
Putty, NSW, 2330
Australia

www.stshenoudamonastery.org.au

ISBN 13: 978-0-9805171-6-3

Cover Design:

Peter Botros,
Bot Dezign Pty Ltd
www.botdezign.com.au.

All scripture quotations, unless otherwise indicated, are taken from the New King James Version. Copyright © 1982 by Thomas Nelson, Inc. Used by permission. All rights reserved.

Contents

Foreword	7
Introduction	9
1. Monasticism, is it an invitation or a duty?	13
2. Some difficulties facing those who wish to become monks	21
3. The blessings of monasticism	27
4. The journey of the monk to the wilderness	31
5. The great test	45
6. The journey of the monk to the wilderness	53
7. The rite of ordaining monks for monasticism	61
8. A day in a monk's life	69
9. The life of solitude in monasticism	77
10. Monasticism and the holy bible	79
11. Monasticism is a continuation of the era of martyrdom	89
12. Monks are faithful soldiers to the lord Jesus Christ	91
13. Monasticism, better than a kingdom	97
14. Monasticism, a Christian philosophy	99
15. Monasticism is a life of repentance	103
16. Monasticism is a life of pilgrimage and death to the world	111
17. Monasticism is a life of consecration	117
18. Monasticism is a life of prayer	119
19. Monasticism is a life of discipleship	129
20. Monasticism is a life of fulfilling the commandments	137
21. Monasticism is a life of preparation for the second coming of the Lord Christ	143
22. Monasticism is an angelic life and a heavenly rite	147
23. Monasticism is a life of spiritual happiness	149
24. The basic fundamentals of monasticism	155
25. Nothing is greater than monasticism	167

Foreword

The Monastic Calling

"Those whom you have shone upon them with your love could not live amongst people" (St. John Saba)

Monasticism is an angelic life and the way of Christian perfection. It's main principles are chastity, obedience, and poverty, and it's goal is attaining salvation and being united with Christ.

Virginity (chastity) leads to a sanctified understanding of human nature and emotions directed towards their creator. Virginity is consecration of the senses for the love of the Holy One, spending one's time in worship, meditation and praise, in imitation of the angels.

Obedience leads to humility, which overcomes one's pride and leads to obedience to God. Submitting your will to the Holy Spirit begins by training yourself to obey your confession father and heeding his advice in the true spirit of discipleship.

Poverty leads to ascetism and gives your spirit the sweet taste of humility. Poverty also provides freedom from materialistic things and helps one to gain spiritual depth.

Monasticism is the Biblical way of attaining Christian perfection as the monk spends his time analysing himself and working on his weaknesses in the light of the Bible's commandments.

Monasticism is the link between the struggling church and the victorious church as monks are heavenly beings or earthly angels, "you gave those who are on earth the praise of the cherubim" (from the liturgy of St. Gregory).

The funeral prayer is prayed on the monk during his ordination so as to lift him from the earthly to a heavenly life. For this reason many people left the world and their family and lived in the deserts and caves longing for this life, the life of Christian perfection.

In this generation many books were published about the lives of these monks which drew many youth to the monastic life. Always one question is repeated "What are the signs of the monastic calling?"

This book contains many spiritual experiences of a monk who has tasted the sweetness of this life in the wilderness of Scetis and I hope that through this book you will find the answer to this question.

We pray that God may bless the monastic life in our church through the prayers of H.H. Pope Shenouda III, the father of all monks of our days, who encourages monasticism and returned it to it's glorious days.

Through the prayers of H.G. Bishop Theophilus, the Bishop of El-Syrian Monastery, who dedicated his life to the service of the monastic life in the wilderness of Scetis for over 50 years until this wilderness flourished with a large number of monks.

May God bless the author of this book and make him as a fruitful tree that is planted by the riverside.

H.E. Bishop Bishoy,
Metropoleten of Dimiatte &
the Monastery of St Demiana
First Edition 1975

INTRODUCTION

I write this introduction in my cell at the Syrian Monastery on my 25th anniversary as a monk. How happy I am and how can I thank the Lord for all his gifts and blessings that can not be expressed.

On my 25th anniversary, I stop and contemplate on God's mercy towards me and His mighty hand that is good upon me (Nehemiah 2:18). It is He who made my unworthiness go to the monastery and become a monk and Who also has taken care of me all these years and saturated me with His love. I therefore feel joyful and am thankful towards my God the Lover of mankind. I pray that He may complete my struggle in peace on the path of my forefathers the saints, who have pleased the Lord with their righteous deeds and were worthy to receive the everlasting crowns in eternal life.

Monasticism my beloved, is the royal path that leads to the Kingdom of Heaven. An elder once said, "There is no nation in this world like Christians if they keep the law and there is no higher rank than monks if they keep their laws". Also St John the Short once said, "Let us appreciate the great honour that we (monks) have in front of God".

A monk is a person who strives to be like angels. A monk is the person in whom the love of the world has died in their heart and who says with St Paul, "But God forbid that I should boast except in the cross of our Lord Jesus

Christ, by whom the world has been crucified to me, and I to the world." (Galatians 6:14)

The rite of ordination of new monks reveals how a monk should live, what the monastic calling is all about and how to live it properly.

A monk is a person who died from the world and at their ordination the funeral prayer is prayed on them as well as the Litany of the departed. All chants are in the sad funeral tunes.

A monk is the person who is likened to our great father Abraham who listened to the voice of God and left his land and fathers house and went to the monastery God had chosen. There he can worship Him and live according to His commandments. As a reward God blesses him and he becomes a blessing to the church and the whole world. (Genesis 12:1-8)

A monk is the person on whom is done what is written in Leviticus 8:1-9, "And the Lord spoke to Moses, saying: "Take Aaron and his sons with him, and the garments, the anointing oil, a bull as the sin offering, two rams, and a basket of unleavened bread; and gather all the congregation together at the door of the tabernacle of meeting. "So Moses did as the Lord commanded him. And the congregation was gathered together at the door of the tabernacle of meeting. And Moses said to the congregation, "This is what the Lord commanded to be done." Then Moses brought Aaron and his sons and washed them with water. And he put the tunic on him, girded him with the sash, clothed him with the robe, and put the ephod on him; and he girded him with the intricately woven band of the ephod, and with it tied the ephod on him. Then he put the breastplate on him, and he put the Urim and the Thummim in the breastplate. And he put the turban on his head. Also on the turban, on its front, he put the golden plate, the holy crown, as the Lord had commanded Moses."

A monk keeps God's commandments and they become food for his soul. He obeys God's commandments so that he may be granted eternal life in the heavenly Jerusalem.

A monk is the person who perseveres in righteousness and trains himself in patience and perseverance as Jesus Son of Sirach says, "My son, if you come forward to serve the Lord, prepare yourself for temptation. Set your heart right and be steadfast, and do not be hasty in time of calamity. Cleave to him and do not depart, that you may be honoured at the end of your life. Accept whatever is brought upon you, and in changes that humble you be patient. For gold is tested in the fire, and acceptable men in the furnace of humiliation. Trust in him, and he will help you; make your ways straight, and hope in him. You who fear the Lord, wait for his mercy; and turn not aside, lest you fall. You who fear the Lord, trust in him, and your reward will not fail; you who fear the Lord, hope for good things, for everlasting joy and mercy." (Jesus Son of Sirach 2:1-9)

A monk is the person who holds on to God in his struggle as St Paul said, "Finally, my brethren, be strong in the Lord and in the power of His might. Put on the whole armor of God, that you may be able to stand against the wiles of the devil. For we do not wrestle against flesh and blood, but against principalities, against powers, against the rulers of the darkness of this age, against spiritual hosts of wickedness in the heavenly places. Therefore take up the whole armor of God, that you may be able to withstand in the evil day, and having done all, to stand. Stand therefore, having girded your waist with truth, having put on the breastplate of righteousness, and having shod your feet with the preparation of the gospel of peace; above all, taking the shield of faith with which you will be able to quench all the fiery darts of the wicked one. And take the helmet of salvation, and the sword of the Spirit, which is the word of God; praying always with all prayer and supplication in the Spirit, being watchful to this end with all perseverance and supplication for all the saints -- and for me, that utterance may be given to me, that I may open my mouth boldly to make known the mystery of the gospel, for which I am an ambassador in chains; that in it I may speak boldly, as I ought to speak." (Ephesians 6:10-20)

A monk is the person who loves God more than anything and everyone, even himself. He must have such deep love for God to be worthy of following Christ in this angelic life, as is read from the Gospel during the ordination of monks; "When He had called the people to Himself, with His disciples also, He said to them, "Whoever desires to come after Me, let him deny himself, and take up his cross, and follow Me. For whoever desires to save his life will lose it, but whoever loses his life for My sake and the gospel's will save it. For what will it profit a man if he gains the whole world, and loses his own soul? Or what will a man give in exchange for his soul? For whoever is ashamed of Me and My words in this adulterous and sinful generation, of him the Son of Man also will be ashamed when He comes in the glory of His Father with the holy angels." (Mark 8:34-38)

A monk is the person who puts aside his worldly thoughts and consecrates his thoughts on God alone. This is why a monks hair is cut in the shape of a cross by the bishop during ordination, symbolising that the monk has cut off all the old thoughts of the world so that new holy thoughts may grow instead.

The soul of the monk who completes his monastic struggle, holding fast to its principles, rejoices being in the presence of God and when it departs from his body he hears these beautiful words, "In all your ways acknowledge Him, And He shall direct your paths." (Proverbs 3:6) and also, "O you simple ones, understand prudence, And you fools, be of an understanding heart." (Proverbs 8:5). "A little sleep, a little slumber, A little folding of the hands to sleep" (Proverbs 6:10). When he finally goes to heaven he hears the joyful voice, "His lord said to him, "Well done, good and faithful servant; you were faithful over a few things, I will make you ruler over many things. Enter into the joy of your lord.'" (Matthew 25:21).

We have reprinted this book for the third time after the previous editions were sold out and many requests were made to reprint it.

We hope that this new edition is a source of blessing for the readers and a source of spiritual growth and encouragement to the monastic life.

Through the pleadings of our holy Virgin St Mary and the prayers of H.H. Pope Shenouda III the head of all monks.

Glory be to God. Amen.

H.G. Bishop Mettaous
General Bishop
Jonah's Fast February 1990

1. Monasticism, Is it a Vocation or a Duty?

The question of whether monasticism is a vocation or a duty is a question that is frequently asked by spiritual youth and zealous servants who want to please their Creator yet are unsure of their calling. They want to hear God's voice in their life, chanting with the Psalmist ; "Cause me to hear Your loving kindness in the morning, For in You do I trust; Cause me to know the way in which I should walk, For I lift up my soul to You. Deliver me, O Lord, from my enemies; In You I take shelter. Teach me to do Your will, For You are my God; Your Spirit is good. Lead me in the land of uprightness." (Psalm 143:8-10), and with Moses the Prophet; "Now therefore, I pray, if I have found grace in Your sight, show me now Your way, that I may know You and that I may find grace in Your sight. And consider that this nation is Your people." (Exodus 33:13). They are seeking which mode of life is best for the salvation of their souls, whether it is through monasticism for a life of prayer and worship, or priesthood providing pastoral care in the world, or celibacy to dedicate one's life for service in the world, or marriage having a blessed Christian family and an exemplary house as that of Priscilla and Aquila. Here, we will try to highlight the monastic vocation, which may answer some of the questions that the youth have asked and relieve those who are confused.

THE VOCATION AND CHOICE

If we want to know the Holy Bible's teaching concerning the calling and choice for monasticism, we need to first examine St. Paul's Epistle to the Romans, where he states; "For whom He foreknew, He also predestined to be conformed to the image of His Son, that he might be the firstborn among many brethren. Moreover whom He predestined, these He also called; whom He called, these He also justified; and whom He justified, these He also glorified." (Romans 8:29-30). Although in this passage the Apostle is referring to salvation, we can also apply this verse to monasticism. For whom He foreknew, He also predestined... Moreover, whom He predestined, these He also called. We notice here that knowing them precedes predestining them, which is followed by calling and inviting them. This indicates that choosing and calling depends on foreknowing, which means that God knew them through His Divine and unlimited knowledge, predestined them to accept His calling and as such saw in them the potential for a life of prayer and worship and consequently called them to monasticism.

Those whom He saw were ready for priesthood are called for this blessing and so forth. This is because God knows everything before it occurs, everyone before birth, "O Lord, You have searched me and known me. You know my sitting down and my rising up; You understand my thought afar off. You comprehend my path and my lying down, and are acquainted with all my ways. For there is not a word on my tongue, but behold O Lord, You know it altogether. You have hedged me behind and before, and laid Your hand upon me. Such knowledge is too wonderful for me; it is high, I cannot attain it." (Psalm 139:1-6), "For you have formed my inward parts; You covered me in my mother's womb. I will praise You, for I am fearfully and wonderfully made; Marvellous are Your works, And that my soul knows very well. My frame was not hidden from you, when I was made in secret, And skilfully wrought in the lowest parts on the earth. Your eyes saw my substance, being yet unformed. And in Your book they all were written, The days fashioned for me, When as yet there were none of them." (Psalm 139:13-16). David also says in another Psalm; "The Lord looks from heaven; He sees all the sons of men. From the place of His dwelling He looks on all the inhabitants of the earth; He fashions the hearts individually; He considers all their works." (Psalm 33:13-15).

God therefore knows the future in exactly the same way as He knows the past, and He knows the abilities and circumstances of each person and knows them by their name; "Then Moses said to the Lord, 'See, You say to me, 'Bring up this people.' But You have not let me know whom You will send with me.

1. Monasticism, Is it a Vocation or a Duty

Yet You have said, 'I know you by name, and you have also found grace in My sight.'" (Exodus 33:12).

HOW CAN A PERSON KNOW THAT THEY ARE CALLED TO MONASTICISM?

It is possible to discern whether a person is called to monasticism through self-testing and if he/she has the following inclinations: A great love for the life of celibacy and an enormous yearning for its crown. Admiration for celibacy in our Lord Jesus' life, the Virgin St. Mary, Old Testament Prophets such as Elijah, Elisha and Jeremiah. The blessing of celibacy of St. John and St. Paul the Apostles.Special admiration and meditations on the verses calling for and praising celibacy, as our Lord Jesus says: "All cannot accept this saying, but only those to whom it has been given" (considering celibacy a precious gift and perfect gift from above, coming down from the Father of Lights) "For there are eunuchs who were born thus from their mother's womb, and there are eunuchs who were made eunuchs by men, and there are eunuchs who have made themselves eunuchs for the kingdom of heaven's sake." (Matthew 19:11-12). To love and meditate on St. Paul's words "Now concerning the things of which you wrote to me: it is good for a man not to touch a woman." (1 Corinthians 7:1) "But I say to the unmarried and to the widows: it is good for them if they remain even as I am." (1 Corinthians 7:8). "But he who is married cares about the things of the world, how he may please his wife. There is a difference between a wife and a virgin. The unmarried woman cares about the things of the Lord, that she may be holy both in body and in spirit. But she who is married cares about the things of the world, how she may please her husband. And this I say for your own profit, not that I may put a leash on you, but for what is proper, and that you may serve the Lord without distraction." (1 Corinthians 7: 33-35).

- He/she might find special interest in reading the spiritual books dealing with celibacy or the blessing of monasticism.

- Does not suffer any suppression or indirectness of thought or behaviour.

- Living in inner purity, in terms of mind, body and spirit, or at least in readiness to strive for purity.

- Although he/she knows that marriage is holy, he/she prefers celibacy and monasticism in order to reach perfection, as the Apostle says; "So then he who gives her in marriage does well, but he who does not give her in marriage does better." (1 Corinthians 7:38).

1. Renunciation of money, position, fame etc. as one of the saints said; "If you want to be known to God, try not to be known and recognized by the people."

2. Be prepared to renounce those to whom he/she is emotionally connected, such as one's family, relatives and friends, preferring Jesus' love and community. As the Lord Jesus says: "He who loves father or mother more than Me is not worthy of Me. And he who loves son or daughter more than me is not worthy of Me." (Matthew 10: 37).

3. Loves meditation, solitude, prayers and enjoys being free to spend time with the Lord Jesus, considering it better than any pastime providing sweet satisfaction for one's life. St. Isaac the Syrian says: "He who loves Christ, loves to sit alone all the time in his cell."

4. Ready to always be silent, possessing a love of quietness and stillness and an ability to abstain from mixing with people or listening to nonsense.

5. Be prepared to tolerate and be longsuffering. If he/she is to fulfil the commandment of love that is serving and sacrificing, he/she also has to practice and fulfil the commandment of longsuffering in monasticism, which is higher than the first. As the Lord Jesus says; "And he who does not take his cross and follow after Me is not worthy of Me." (Matthew 10:38), and also: "By your patience possess your souls." (Luke 21:19).

6. Be prepared to obey any order relating to work that needs to be done, quick to apologise for any mistakes made, humble and easy to deal with. From personal experience, he/she who does not possess these virtues is destroyed by monasticism.

7. Fasting, piety, asceticism and renouncing possessions. As the Apostle says; "And having food and clothing, with these we shall be content." (1 Timothy 6:8).

All of the aforementioned points are for a person who is spiritually developed and yearns to reach perfection through monasticism, away from the busy troubled world. But as for the person who lives in the world struggling to overcome difficult sins and failing to do so, either because of their weak will or because of the sovereignty of sin over them, or because they are living in a defiled atmosphere at home where it is difficult to live a life of repentance and holiness, it becomes an urgent duty to direct themselves to monasticism for the sake of their salvation.

FLYING TO THE WILDERNESS:

- He forsakes the fatal and corrupt atmosphere surrounding him, which will kill his soul and send it to eternal destruction.
- To live in the holy pure wilderness, searching for virtues and blessings and following in the monks footsteps. There in the monastery, he lives the life of repentance and striving for his/her salvation.

EXAMPLES OF MONASTIC CALLINGS:

One of the fathers said: "Before graduating, I always dreamt of having a happy family, wife and children. Following graduation, I was unable to find a suitable job, so I continued to pray to God and became closer to Him. Finally, I got an excellent position, where I met a colleague who was a faithful servant with monastic intentions. I began serving with him, reading lots of spiritual books, and developed an idea about celibacy and its advantages for the youth. Gradually, the idea of marriage started to vanish. Later, I met another friend who was also planning to join the monastery and who talked a lot about monasticism and eventually, he left for the monastery and became a monk. We continued sending letters to each other and he used to encourage me by advising me to not back out of this blessed intention. Two years later, after thinking deeply and yielding the matter into God's hands, I decided to go and spend my holiday in the monastery. There God prepared me for a meeting with one of the righteous fathers. We talked for hours and he eased all the matters that I perceived as problems facing my monasticism. I eventually resigned from work, took all my spiritual books and belongings, joined the monastery and became a monk.

Another father said: "I deeply loved monasticism after reading "The Life of Orthodox Prayer" released by El Syrian Monastery for the first edition. At that time, I was still in High School. I loved prayers, solitude and retreats, obtaining great comfort, peace and joy when spending time with the Lord. As I waited for the high school certificate results, I dreamt of myself asking the school's secretary about my results. The Lord answered and said "Why do you worry about the results, aren't you going to be a monk?" I woke up the following morning comforted and encouraged. I entered university, graduated and got a job. In all honesty, my monastic intentions persevered and protected me during this critical stage of my youth, where many youths get dragged into bad habits, failure and destruction. During this period, I would go to the monastery frequently. Finally, I decided to go to the monastery and become a monk, but after a few days, I was defeated by some thoughts. I left the monastery and went back to the world, trying to free my intellect from the idea of monasticism. One day, I tried to jump into a tram while it was slowing down and fell under the wheels. I heard people screaming, as it was a dreadful accident. However, to everyone's surprise, they pulled me out from under the wheels with minor scratches. Someone later told me that as he was watching, it was as if someone was trying to stop me from getting hit by the tram wheels. After this accident, I returned to my old vow of monasticism with the Lord. I thought that if monasticism is death from the world, it is better for me to die under the feet of Christ. I considered this accident as a sign from the Lord to fulfil my vow, as King Solomon says; "Better not to vow than to vow and not pay." (Ecclesiastes 5:5). A few days later, I went back to the monastery, living in obedience to God, in happiness with the community. "I have been crucified with Christ; it is no longer I who live, but Christ lives in me; and the life which I now live in the flesh I live by faith in the Son of God, who loved me and gave Himself for me." (Galatians 2:20).

A third story by a monk is as follows: "I was a solider in the army and became involved in the war. As the enemy began shooting at my comrades and I, we laid down facing the ground and I felt, heard and saw the bullets passing over my head. At that moment, I prayed to God and asked for St. Mary's intercession, vowing to give my life in the service of the Lord in whatever way He finds suitable for me. I found a hand covering my head, which protected me from the bullets, while everyone around me was screaming, wounded or killed. When the war came to an end and my military service was completed, I was unable to find within myself any potential for service in the world, so I fulfilled my vow and became a monk."

A fourth monk recounts: "I wanted to become a monk, however, my parents refused and instead, forced me to get married. After a brief period of time, my wife died, and the idea of monasticism again entered my mind, and again, my parents refused. I then fell sick and was on the brink of death, to the extent that a rotten stench came from my body, and I was diagnosed as a hopeless case. However the kind and tender Lord had mercy on me, and I was healed. My parents then said to me: 'If monasticism is death to the world, we already saw you dying and your body rot. Since you have been granted new life, go and spend it with God in the monastery.' I then went to the monastery and became a monk."

THE REASON FOR THE FAILURE OF SOME MONKS

At times we hear of monks who quit monasticism by breaking their vow and going back into the world. Some may get married, while others may regret their decision and return to the monastery. If this is the case, they are not re-ordained as monks, but rather, they return as a monk, on the condition that they are accepted back into the monastery.

SOME REASONS FOR QUITTING MONASTICISM

The strictness of the family environment may entice some youths to enter the monastery, or a refusal for them to marry the person they choose, or forcing them to marry a person they do not love. In these cases, the youth's last resort is to enter the monastery, pretending to be spiritual and obedient. After a while, they find the life of isolation and spiritual warfare unbearable and they return to the world in great shame.

Some young men came to the monastery in search for clerical positions and leadership positions in the church. On failing to fulfil this, they withdraw.

Others, begin with the genuine intention and with a holy vocation to monasticism, but they may also withdraw because of their reluctance to follow the monastery's rules concerning prayers, fasting, praises etc. as set by the Holy Spirit through the early fathers. God respects our freedom to choose whatever suits us. We have many examples in the Bible about people of whom it was said, "Are you so foolish? Having begun in the Spirit, are you now being made perfect by the flesh?" (Galatians 3:3), also others; "But the Pharisees and lawyers rejected the will of God for themselves, not having been baptised by Him." (Luke 7:30). These people started in the Spirit, but then relinquished their vow as Judas Iscariot, who loved money more than his Master and finally left the Lord and the disciples. Also, Nicholas the deacon, who relinquished his vow and led others to the Nicolaitans heresy, which the Lord also despises. There is also Demas, one of St. Paul's disciples who abandoned the service for love of the world. Such monks suffer spiritual coldness and boredom, as they do not heed the monastic calling, but rather interfere in everything, they like to hear the news and stories about others and like to be leaders. Eventually, these people return to the world.

2. Some Difficulties Facing Those Who Wish to Become Monks

While a person may feel that they have a desire to monasticism and that this lifestyle is the most suitable for them, they are faced with some obstacles and difficulties which will now be discussed.

Fearing the Unknown Future

In spite of visiting the monastery frequently and spending a great deal of time there, the monastic life remains a great mystery to many. This problem may be solved by spending more time at the monastery, meeting with spiritual fathers who are able to explain everything in a monk's daily life, monasticism and its philosophy, etc.

Fearing the loss of one's initial love for monasticism

Such thoughts reflect a lack of faith in God's power and grace. A person who feels the invitation to monasticism should submit their life into God's hands, as only He is capable of remaining with them till the end; "With men this is impossible, but with God all things are possible." (Matthew 19:26). The Apostle also says; "For this reason I also suffer these things; nevertheless I am not ashamed, for I know whom I have believed and am persuaded that He is able to keep what I have committed to Him until that Day." (2 Timothy 1:12). Moreover, the Lord comforts the soul that leaves everything and is seeking His love and community.

FEARING BOREDOM

Some youth do not know exactly what monastic life is and are under the impression that a monk does nothing, and lives in total emptiness! On the contrary, a true monk is the busiest of persons. He is busy with the Lord Jesus who fills his heart and soul so that there is no room for emptiness or boredom. In addition to all the bodily and spiritual daily activities, the monks occupy their time with:

- The Agpia Prayers which consist of the 1st, 3rd, 6th, 9th, 11th, 12th hour, and the Veil (with its many Psalms) and the Midnight Prayer with its three services. The Agpia Prayers are a very special canon for every monk and are to be prayed inside his cell on a daily basis.

- The Midnight Praise with its beautiful tunes and hymns, prayed daily with other monks in the church following the Midnight Prayer, or alone in his cell.

- The Holy Liturgy which is prayed in the monastery daily or some days of the week. The monk attends as regularly as he can and partakes of the Holy Communion in order to strengthen his spiritual life.

- The metania canon, according to his agreement with his spiritual father and is to be done each morning, asking for God's mercy.

- Readings in the Holy Bible daily for nourishment.

- "Jesus Prayer" or any short prayer of the monk's choice, to be repeated continuously or as much as possible.

- Reading the lives of the Saints who preceded him, and their sayings, in order to attain comfort from them and follow in their steps. "Remember those who rule over you, who have spoken the word of God to you, whose faith follow, considering the outcome of their conduct." (Hebrews 13: 7).

2. Some Difficulties Facing Those Who Wish to Become Monks

- The handwork appointed to him by the monastery, either in the kitchen, the bakery, the church or the library. Each monk is given a job as this helps in the development of his spirituality, in addition to giving him a variety of things to do, including his own personal chores such as washing etc.
- Serving the other monks, the sick or those who need help. He can also teach hymns and praises.
- Copying old manuscripts, writing books on deep spiritual meditations, translation, studying the Coptic language in depth.
- Making leather crosses while reciting psalms and prayers.

Fear of the Lack of Spiritual Guides in the Monastery

Truly, at a certain stage, monasticism went through a dry period, where there were rarely any spiritual guides. However, we thank God that it is flourishing again and there are now many experienced fathers, whose spiritual fruits have begun to appear.

Family Ties

The major problem for a person who wants to become a monk is how to inform their desire to their family and how they will tolerate living apart from them. While it is beautiful to love your family and to be loved by them in return, if you have a desire for monasticism, God should be obeyed more than people. Christ's love should come before any other love. "He who loves father or mother more than Me is not worthy of Me. And he who loves son or daughter more than Me is not worthy of Me." (Matthew 10:37). Parents prevent their children from going to the monastery by using the excuse that they are unable to tolerate being separated from them, while they let them migrate to America, Australia, Europe etc. where it is difficult to see them frequently. In this respect, they can bear the separation if the motive is to get rich, but they are unable to bear it if it has to do with entering the monastery, to spend one's life in God's service. Another common attitude is that some youths go to foreign countries for study or work and get married there and return with their foreign wives. In these cases, I wonder that this wife, for the love of her husband, has left her country, her family and friends and all that she had to come with her husband and live in a completely different and at times strange atmosphere. She is able to tolerate everything because she loves her husband, while we are unable to sacrifice for the sake of the Groom, the Beloved Lord Jesus and for our eternal salvation. Truly, the Lord says; "So the master commended the unjust steward because he had dealt shrewdly. For the sons of this world are more shrewd in their generation than the sons of light." (Luke 16:8). The parental love, which forbids a person from God's love and consecration, fulfils the verse; "and a man's enemies will be those of his own household."(Matthew 10:36).

THE LOVE OF POSITIONS

If the person is in a respectable job and a high position, it can at times become a reason for hindering the call of monasticism. In this case, a person needs to meditate in the joy and happiness of eternity, with our Lord Christ in heaven and consider St. Paul's words; "But what things were gain to me, these I have counted loss for Christ. Yet indeed I also count all things loss for the excellence of the knowledge of Christ Jesus my Lord, for whom I have suffered the loss of all things, and count them as rubbish, that I may gain Christ and be found in Him, not having my own righteousness, which is from the law, but that which is through faith in Christ, the righteousness which is from God by faith." (Philippians 3:7-9).

THE RESPONSIBILITIES OF THE SERVICE

If the person is a Sunday School servant, they at times, can become so involved in the service, that others might convince him that they are essential to the service and they are a source of blessing to many etc.. This person should know that if they go to the monastery, they will also be fruitful and a blessing to the whole church, not just a class or to one branch of the service. While the servants are busy with their service, they do not have enough time to pray for the salvation of themselves and those whom they serve. In monasticism they will be consecrated for the service of praying for them. Martha was serving Jesus but Mary was sitting under His feet hearing his words. While Joshua was fighting Amalek, Moses was praying on the mountain, raising up his hands. In the same way that the church needs people for service, it also needs people for prayers. When your colleagues in the service and the children whom you used to serve know that you have gone to the monastery, they will benefit from your love and ascetic life more than your words. They might follow your example while in the world by their love of God and spirituality. The Lord Jesus says; "Most assuredly, I say unto you, unless a grain of wheat falls into the ground and dies, it remains alone; but if it dies, it produces much grain." (John 12:24). The disciples did not believe in the Lord's words until He died and resurrected; "The other disciple, who came to the tomb first, went in also; and he saw and believed." (John 20:8).

THE RESPONSIBILITY OF YOUR CHILDREN'S SALVATION

In some cases, a servant may use the following excuse: "I cannot leave my children, their salvation is my entire responsibility." It is wonderful that they feel this way, but remember my beloved, you are not the only one responsible for their salvation. The priest, head of service and family also share this responsibility. If you feel the call for monasticism, you can delegate your class to another servant or to the head of service to appoint the appropriate servant for the class and you should go and heed the call. You can still serve your children from the depth of the wilderness, by praying for each of them. You are merely changing the means of service.

THE RESPONSIBILITY OWARDS THE FAMILY

At times, the person may be the only one who is caring for the family after the departure of the father, or they have not completed their military recruitment obligation or other commitments of this nature. In such cases, it is preferable to wait until everything has settled down. The monastery does not accept a person who has failed in his studies, professional life, family care, etc.

THE CONFESSION FATHER'S OBJECTION

I think that the confession fathers would never prevent a person who is really longing for monasticism. However, they may clarify things for them, explaining the hardships of the life that they will face, their responsibility towards the family etc... At times the father confessor may observe or test the persons true will. The mature youth has to convince their confession father that they are sincere in their intention. If the father confessor is certain of his/her decision for monasticism, he would not object, knowing that if he objected or prevented him without an adequate reason and was acting in this manner out of his spiritual authority, he will be responsible for this **before** God, particularly if the youth's spiritual life weakened as a result of living in the world, feeling that they have not achieved their aim of monasticism.

3. The Blessings of Monasticism

There are many blessings accompanying the monastic call and angelic life, not only for the monk, but also extending to the house, the church and to the whole world.

For the Person Joining Monasticism

A youth who is able to escape the world, with all its disturbances, evils and responsibilities and enter the monastery, has successfully started a way to reach God. If he lives a simple life of repentance, in honesty, asceticism, always looking to the heavenly Jerusalem, he will undoubtedly find the way to God.

For their family

Initially the family will miss their loved one going to the monastery because of family ties but when they accept the intention and bless and pray for them, their sadness will be turned into joy. They will wish that they could be on the same level of asceticism and spirituality. At times, if the monks parents, family and relatives are busy with the world and its pleasures, they begin thinking more seriously about eternal life and change their relationship with God, giving Him His share of their time, money and life, living the life of repentance.

The parents are proud to offer their son or daughter to the Lord, who will be praying and interceding on their behalf and this gives them joy. The whole family experiences the blessing of having one of its members as a monk or nun, financially and spiritually.

For the Church

The monks and nuns are the hidden line in the church's army. The church is indebted to them for maintaining its doctrine and spiritual treasures. Many examples exist in history of Popes and bishops who resorted to monasteries in times of persecution, asking for the prayers of the monks and divine help. Many churches were burnt or robbed destroying precious books and scripts, yet we still have many of these preserved in the monasteries. It is recorded that when Alexandria's Theological College was closed, all the teachers and students went to St. Macarius monastery. The monks there protected those theologians.

Monasticism enriched the church with lives of saints and fatherly sayings, which are so sublime and spiritual. The church is still nourished by these teachings and sayings. Many monks became martyrs and saints; they joined the victorious church, praying for it in times of struggle. We notice that most of the monks were previously responsible and honest servants, often serving Christ and his children in the church. They go out to the wilderness to serve Christ directly through prayers, praises and meditations. We see St. Paul's disciple after teaching and serving honestly the Colossians; "as you also learned from Epaphras, our dear fellow servant, who is a faithful minister of Christ on your behalf." (Colossians 1:7). He is struggling in prayers for this church and other churches; "Epaphras, who is one of you, a bondservant of Christ, greets you, always labouring fervently for you in prayers, that you may stand perfect and complete in all the will of God. For I bear him witness that he has a great zeal for you, and those who are in Laodicea, and for those in Hierapolis." (Colossians 4:12-13). St. Athanasius the Apostolic says: "If monasticism is strong, the church too will be strong, but if monasticism starts to weaken, consequently, the church will become weak."

For the Whole World

A true monk or nun is actually a blessing for the whole world. One of the elderly fathers said, "The world sees God with the eyes of men of prayers, it breathes eternity through the lungs of spiritual people, walks towards heaven

3. The Blessings of Monasticism

through the feet of those who are fasting." Bishop Poemen says in his book The Life of Chastity; "The monks are chosen from among the whole world, the Holy Spirit descended on them, and the world is sanctified through them. The monks are like the harvest and the first born of the cattle offered to God, so He blesses all the harvest and the cattle. They are like the yeast which raises the whole dough. A married person gives fruits but on a limited scale. A celibate and a monk give fruits on a wider scale, having no limits because the whole world is their vineyard." p.109)

It is a fact that St. Macarius had many foreign disciples, so in the 4th Doxology we sing "… that is why they used to come to you from the end of the world, from Rome, Syria, the East and Spain..." St. Macarius was the spiritual father of saints Maximos and Domadios, the sons of king Valentianous. Even after his death, all those from all over the world who were looking for an ascetic life used to head for his wilderness, and after being disciples to the great Egyptian saints, they went back to their countries and became great monks, fathers, bishops and popes.

There were many foreigners who became monks in Egypt and we still have "El Syrian Monastery", which derived its name from the monks coming from Syria. There are also monuments of the Armenian and Ethiopian monasteries near El Syrian monastery and many foreign monks were disciples to St. Pachomius the father of the community, where they lived in groups according to their nationalities and languages.

In The Paradise of The Holy Fathers we read about St. Isaiah of Scetis, who once stood almost naked in the sun praying for the whole world. One of the monks heard a voice saying, "Go and give St. Isaiah a robe to cover his body because I had mercy on the whole world because of his prayers". Also in this book, there is a story about one of the monks who, during a famine, had only three dry loaves of bread left. Someone came and knocked at his door asking for bread, so the monk gave him two loaves. When it was time to break his daily fasting and eat, another person knocked, so he gave him his third loaf. He remained hungry without food for three days. He then heard a voice saying, "there will be no more famines on earth during your life." A person then came carrying lots of food sent to him from a nearby village. We also hear that it rained heavily after a long period of drought because of the prayers of St. Macarius of Alexandria and also St. Jacob the Repentant on another occasion.

The monks are always a blessing to the whole world. People visit monasteries and get great comfort and blessing, either merely by the look of the monks or their speech, or by meditating on their philosophy of life. My dear brethren, ask God to reveal to you His goal in your life, test your inner self accurately and always pray.

HAVING A CLEAR VIEW AFTER PERSISTING IN PRAYER AND PATIENCE

After many tests and spiritual advice, you will be able to discern God's will in your life, whether it be monasticism or priesthood. If you are not comfortable to make the decision yet, keep working in whatever profession you are practicing, in complete honesty, until the Lord guides you and your direction in life is changed according to his Divine Providence.

Some Advice by St. Clement to those seeking monasticism

- The level of monasticism is that of angels, who never cease in praising their Creator. He who is reluctant after being a monk, is in a worse situation than if he is living on the same level of reluctance in the world.

- A monk is the person who is prepared to live as an angel and tear off the robe of the world and its lust.

- Never ignore any minor or major commandment, but fulfil all of them steadily, otherwise it is best that you live with the laymen.

4. The Journey of the Monk to the Wilderness

The Journey of the monk into the wilderness is the same as the journey of the children of Israel in the Sinai desert. God likes us to worship Him in the wilderness, in order to have the opportunity to taste Him and cling to Him. When God ordered Moses to take the children of Israel out of Egypt, He said to Moses; "I will certainly be with you. And this shall be a sign to you that I have sent you: When you have bought the people out of Egypt, you shall serve God on this mountain." (Exodus 3:12).

The central aim of the Book of Exodus, the miracles, the commandments etc. is to worship God in the wilderness, a pure undefiled worship. So when Moses and Aaron went to Pharaoh they said to him; "Thus says the Lord God of Israel: 'Let my people go, that they may hold a feast for me in the wilderness.' And Pharaoh said, 'Who is the Lord, that I should obey His voice to let Israel go? I do not know the Lord, nor will I let Israel go.' So they said, 'The God of the Hebrews has met with us. Please, let us go three days' journey into the desert and sacrifice to the Lord our God, lest He fall upon us with pestilence or with the sword.'" (Exodus 5:1-3). Pharaoh refused so Moses said; "But if you refuse to let them go, behold I will smite all your territory with frogs." (Exodus 8:2), i.e. in the land of Egypt. Pharaoh strongly refused and Moses said; "It is not right to do so, for we would be sacrificing the abomination of the Egyptians to the Lord our God. If we sacrifice the abomination of the Egyptians before their eyes, then will they not stone us? We will go three days' journey into the wilderness and sacrifice to the Lord our God as He will command us" (Exodus 8: 26-27). Finally Pharaoh said; "I will let you go, that you may sacrifice to the Lord your God in the wilderness; only you shall not go very far away. Intercede for me." (Exodus 8:28).

The wilderness was the preferable place for our Lord Jesus Christ, the Incarnate God. He used to spend a great deal of time in the mountains and wilderness of Palestine. The mountain had frequently witnessed the fervent prayers of our Lord Jesus. His sighs were heard, addressing the Father, as an intercession for the wicked world and as a defender of fallen humanity. On many occasions, during the night and in solitude, there was communion between The Son and The Father at night; "And when He had sent them away, He departed to the mountain to pray." (Mark 6:46). "Now it came to pass in those days that He went out to the mountain to pray, and continued all night in prayer to God." (Luke 6:12). "So He Himself often withdrew into the wilderness and prayed." (Luke 5:16). Undoubtedly, the mountain was full of angels serving Jesus and praising their Humble Creator, "Then the devil left Him, and behold, angels came and ministered to Him." (Matthew 4:11).

Jesus is the meek Son in the mountains; "The voice of my Beloved! Behold, he comes Leaping upon the mountains, Skipping upon the hills." (Song of Songs 2:8), "Make haste, my beloved, and be like a gazelle or a young stag on the mountains of spices." (Song of Songs 8:14). The saints knew that the Lord is always pleased with worship in the wilderness, they followed the steps of Christ, the Teacher of pure prayers, who left us an example to follow (1 Peter 2:21), so they headed towards the wilderness, they inhabited the caves, which later became thousands of churches and monasteries, where the prayers and praises proceed from their lips, pleasing the Lord in heaven.

Advantages of Worship In the Wilderness

1. The wilderness, with its purity and chastity, resembles the Holy of Holies of the world. So, if the world is a church, the wilderness is the altar, which is the most holy place in the Church. Thus the monk is the priest of creation, offering continuous sacrifices of praise and prayer to God on the altar of his pure heart. The Lord thus smells the sweet aroma in pleasure. When David the prophet fled from Saul the King, he went to the wilderness of Judah. As he was unable to go to the tabernacle and pray, he considered the wilderness the Holy of

Holies and he sang his lovely, famous psalm; "O God, You are my God; early will I seek You; My soul thirst for You; My flesh longs for You in a dry and thirsty land where there is no water. So I have looked for You in the sanctuary to see Your power and Your glory." (Psalm 63:1-2). This Psalm is titled "A Psalm of David when he was in the wilderness of Judah."

2. The wilderness is rich with its meditations about the greatness of God who created everything with unlimited wisdom and love. When the monk prays Psalm 121; "I will lift up my eyes to the hills, from whence comes my help ..." while walking in the wilderness, he will meditate on the arms of the Lord, stretched as wide as the wilderness, ready to accept any repentant sinner, sustaining those who need help as the Lord promised us; "All that the Father gives Me will come to Me, and the one who comes to Me I will by no means cast out." (John 6:37).

3. A monk comprehends God's greatness through meditation on the different types of rocks, the sand and the strange plants, which grow without cultivation, because God is the one who is looking after them. As David the Psalmist says; "Who covers the heavens with clouds, who prepares rain for the earth, who makes grass to grow on the mountains. He gives to the beast its food and to the young ravens that cry." (Psalm 147: 8-9).

4. A monk can worship the Creator with all his heart, in the serenity and calmness of the wilderness, away from all the noise of the world.

5. The calmness of the wilderness leads to the calmness of the heart and senses, as St. John Saba says; "Silence your mouth for your heart to speak, silence your heart for God to speak." St. Isaac the Syrian also says; "Just the look of the desert kills any worldly thoughts and desires in our souls, thus we yearn more eagerly for God, we want to get closer to Him and finally become united with Him."

6. A monk can live the true life of repentance in the desert. Repentance is the mother of life, the mother of pure accepted prayer. Without repentance God never accepts any struggle, fasting or prayers; "I tell you, no; but unless you repent you will likewise perish." (Luke 13:3). Therefore without repentance no one will be saved.

7. In the wilderness a monk is released from all the bonds of the world

and a soul discovers how trifle the world is. The soul is lifted up to God, the True light, the True love and the True Beauty.

8. In the wilderness a monk can maintain a clean heart and watch his thoughts. This is the greatest thing a person can do as St. Isaac the Syrian said; "Quietness prevents the mind from wandering around in different thoughts and makes old memories fade away." Palladius, the author of "The Paradise of The Holy Fathers" says; "One day, some philosophers came to test monks in the wilderness. They attempted to outrage a monk by saying to him, 'you sinful monk, come here'. The monk approached them, and one of them slapped him across the face, so the monk turned the other cheek. Seeing this, they all bowed down to him and said: 'What do you monks of the wilderness do more than us? You fast, we also fast, you live in purity, we do the same, but why are you superior to us?' So the monk answered, 'We live in great alertness, watching and guiding our thoughts.' The philosophers said, 'This is above our capabilities.'" St. Isaac says; "He who has mastered great virtues like fasting, asceticism and vigil but has failed to master protecting the heart and tongue, is toiling in vain."

9. In the wilderness there is a great lesson for a monk. In order to find your way in the desert you need a guide because there are no streets or signs to follow. Monasticism is the same as a novice monk needs to be guided by an experienced older monk in order to reach the Heavenly Jerusalem safely. If he depends totally on himself he will lose the way. As Job says; "The paths of their way turn aside, they go nowhere and perish." (Job 6:18). Also in Proverbs; "Where there is no counsel, the people fall; but in the multitude of counselors there is safety." (Proverbs 11:14).

10. In the wilderness away from the busy world, a monk can meditate, worship and study the Holy Bible thoroughly, increasing his spiritual knowledge and experience.

A person who genuinely feels the desire for monasticism within his heart, longing for it after hearing God's voice and yearns to abandon the world with its lusts for the sake of sitting at the feet of the Lord, is exactly like the children of Israel when they were burdened with Pharaoh's slavery. It is written; "Therefore they set taskmasters over them to afflict them with their burdens. And they built for Pharaoh supply cities, Pithom and Raamses. But the more they afflicted them, the more they multiplied and grew. And they were in dread of the children of Israel. So the Egyptians made the children of Israel serve with rigor. And they made their lives bitter with hard bondage – in mortar, in brick, and in all manner of service in the field. All their service in which they made them serve was with rigor." (Exodus 1:11-14), then: "Now it happened in the process of time that the king of Egypt died. Then the children of Israel groaned because of the bondage, and they cried out; and their cry came up to God because of the bondage. So God heard their groaning, and God remembered His covenant with Abraham, with Isaac, and with Jacob. And God looked upon the children of Israel, and God acknowledged them." (Exodus 2:23-25).

THE DIFFICULT STEP OF ABANDONING THE WORLD

In the fullness of time, according to God's will, God sent Moses to deliver the children of Israel from slavery and lead them into the wilderness, He said to Moses; "Then they will heed your voice; and you shall come, you and the elders of Israel, to the king of Egypt; and you shall say to him, 'The Lord God of the Hebrews has met with us; and now, please, let us go three days' journey into the wilderness, that we may sacrifice to the Lord our God.' But I am sure that the king of Egypt will not let you go, no, not even by a mighty hand." (Exodus 3:18-19). It is the same for the believer when he feels comforted and completely convinced with the idea of monasticism, the devil (Pharaoh of the intellect) begins fighting him and placing obstacles in his way in an attempt to hinder him from entering the wilderness. At times, the fight comes from his own household, as the Lord Jesus says; "and a man's enemies will be those of his own household." (Matthew 10:36). In order to overcome all these obstacles, he needs a very special grace and support from God.

THE POWER OF GOD'S SUPPORT

When Moses asked Pharaoh to let the children of Israel go to the wilderness to worship their God, Pharaoh refused and even gave orders to his workers; "You shall no longer give the people straw to make brick as before. Let them go and gather straw for themselves. And you shall lay on them the quota of bricks, which they made before. You shall not reduce it. For they are idle; therefore they cry out saying, 'Let us go and sacrifice to our God.' Let more work be laid on the men, that they may labor in it, and let them not regard false words." (Exodus 5:7-9). When Moses complained to the Lord, the Lord said to him: "Now you shall see what I will do to Pharaoh. For with a strong hand he will let them go, and with a strong hand he will drive them out of his land." (Exodus 6:1).

The same thing happens with a person who wants to go to the wilderness for monasticism. People accuse him of trying to get rid of his responsibilities in the world, claiming that he is lazy, or following an illusion or mirage called monasticism and so on. When this person asks for God's support and help, God begins working with His strong outstretched hand, giving this person grace before the eyes of all people. As a consequence they begin to yield and encourage him.

At times, there are specific family circumstances that hinder a person from becoming a monk, for example:

1. A widow with an only son. It is not appropriate for him to leave his mother and go to the monastery. He will not feel comfortable there and the devil will always fight him through his mother.

2. An elderly couple with an only son, as he is their support in their old age. If he leaves them he will continually be thinking of them and this will spoil his relation with God.

3. A brother who is the eldest in a family of many sisters whose father has just died. He is the one responsible for his sisters, otherwise they may be misguided.

4. A older brother of younger brother and sisters, he is the one bringing them up and responsible for them.

In all these cases the persons family needs him, either socially, financially or emotionally therefore he should not make haste to monasticism. If such a person leaves his family and heads to the monastery, then St. Paul's words apply to him. He should at least postpone the idea of going to the monastery until his circumstances change.

But if the family is settled down and none of the above mentioned reasons exist, they just prevent him from going to the monastery out of their emotional love, or because they want him to get married, then this verse is true; "and a man's enemies will be those of his own household." (Matthew 10:36). The worst enemy for a person is the enemy against his salvation, whether they are family or friends. Jesus came and said; "For I have come to set a man against his father, a daughter against her mother, and a daughter-in-law against her mother-in-law." (Matthew 10:35), which means that He came to separate the

4. The Journey of the Monk to the Wilderness

believing person from his unbelieving father. Such people only love their son on the bodily level, not caring for his spiritual salvation. The Lord warned of such love; "Whatever I tell you in the dark, speak in the light; and what you hear in the ear, preach on the housetops. And do not fear those who kill the body but cannot kill the soul. But rather fear Him who is able to destroy both soul and body in hell." (Matthew 10:27-28). In such cases, he has to leave everything behind and follow Jesus, in the narrow gate of monasticism saying; "We ought to obey God rather than men." (Acts 5:29) and "Therefore, from now on, we regard no one according to the flesh." (2Corinthians 5:16). This person shall head towards monasticism with a comfortable heart and conscience, not doubting that he had annoyed his parents or disobeyed them and that these thoughts have been planted by the devil in people's hearts so that they lose their peace.

THE PREPARATION PERIOD

After all the plagues, God told Moses to prepare the Passover; "And thus you shall eat it: with a belt on your waist, your sandals on your feet, and your staff in your hand. So you shall eat it in haste. It is the Lord's Passover." (Exodus 12:11). 'A belt on your waist' is a sign of getting ready to leave everything behind and begin the path of struggle, heading towards God. 'Your sandals on your feet' symbolises a readiness to walk in the Divine path, away from the defiled path of the world, which is full of sin and iniquity; "Children, obey your parents in the Lord, for this is right." (Ephesians 6:1). 'Your staff in your hand' denotes that the journey is hard and long. The staff in your hand is a helper to lean on, a sign of the Cross of our Lord Jesus, which a monk should keep a strong hold of, to ensure that he reaches Canaan safely. 'So you shall eat it in haste', denotes hunger and so the monk should always feel hungry and thirsty for righteousness to God and His Kingdom, as the Lord Jesus says; "Blessed are those who hunger and thirst for righteousness, for they shall be filled." (Matthew 5:6). David also says: "As the deer pants for the water brooks, so pants my soul for You, O God. My soul thirsts for God, for the living God." (Psalm 42:1-2).

A person whose family and social circumstances allow him to become a monk and who feels the strong call in his heart should pray and think deeply asking God's guidance, visiting lots of monasteries, as well as sitting in spiritual meetings with experienced monks. He also needs to read a great deal on the lives of the saints and their sayings in order to enrich his soul and draw strength against the fights of the evil. He needs to be familiar with the fundamental aspects of monasticism, which will now be discussed.

The Life of Celibacy and Purity

He has to live this life while still in the world, keeping his senses pure, watching what he hears, says or reads.

The Life of Ascetism

The monk must only have the essentials in food and clothes and must not be greedy for money, wealth, position, fame etc.

The Life of Prayers

The monk needs to increase his prayers of the Agpia and pray them with depth, knowing that prayer is central to the life of monasticism. He also has to memorise as much as he can of the Psalms, Gospels and other prayers of the Agpia.

Learning the Coptic Language

If he has an opportunity to learn the Coptic language and start learning the Midnight Praise, this would be a great blessing and he can learn the rest in the monastery.

The Life of Solitude

The monk has to start practicing solitude and communicate less with people, concentrating more on readings and mediations.

Fewer Relationships

It is necessary to start to decrease his friendships so that he is not often disturbed. Numerous relationships may be a hindrance and a cause of losing focus on his monastic life.

The Life of Fasting

It is necessary to fast all church fasts, with a reasonable period of abstaining and metanias (prostrations), according to his confession father's instructions. His confession father should be informed about every single incident and thought in his life, especially during the period of fasts. At times a person gets so enthusiastic fasting etc. beyond their capability without guidance and then becomes frustrated. For this reason they should always follow their spiritual guide's instructions.

THE LIFE OF OBEDIENCE

The person must also practice obedience, as he has practiced ascetism in food and money, he must also do the same with his personal opinions and ideas. Obedience and submission are very important in monasticism, in addition to being flexible, respecting the elders, not despising the younger and saying 'I have sinned' when mistaken. The elder monastic fathers taught us two words with which a monk can live in peace, be loved by everyone and be lead to the shore safely:

1. To say, "Yes", if he is asked to do something and
2. To say, "I have sinned", in humility with all his heart when asked why he did a particular act or told that he shouldn't have done an act. Thus everyone will bless him.

THE LIFE OF TOLERANCE AND PATIENCE

The person has to be patient, long suffering and able to tolerate the weaknesses of others in order to overcome all wars. When the path is very clear and the call is true, he should not delay going to the monastery. Let him recall the words of the angel to Lot, (Gen. 29:17), doing as the children of Israel in their exodus from Egypt; "And thus you shall eat it: with a belt on your waist and sandals on your feet, and your staff in your hand. So you shall eat it in haste. This is the Lord's Passover." 'So the people took their dough before it was leavened, having their kneading bowls bound up in their clothes on their shoulders." (Exodus 12:11).

THE EXODUS

The decision to leave the world and fix a date for carrying it out is a very courageous and sometimes difficult one. A person needs great spiritual help which comes from God's divine providence. When he thinks about the beautiful heavenly life of monasticism and the virtues he will attain in the monastery, then the world and all its temptations will vanish before his eyes. He will head to the monastery singing with David the Psalmist; "Oh, that I had wings like a dove! I would fly away and be at rest. Indeed, I would wander far off, and remain in the wilderness. I would hasten my escape from the windy storm and tempest." (Psalm 55:6-8). Here he is like Abraham who, as soon as he heard the Divine call, (Exodus 12:1), he obeyed immediately; "By faith Abraham obeyed when he was called to go out to the place which he would receive as an inheritance. And he went out not knowing where he was going." (Hebrews 11:8). He never hesitated or thought of where he was going, he simply went to follow God, in a place that God had chosen for him. When Abraham made God his abode, he was able to abandon his country. The feeling of being a stranger on earth (which is a monastic virtue) could not be heeded unless the person feels that he is living in heaven.

The Spiritual Aspect of the Monk's Exodus from the World

The great spiritual power accompanying the monk when first heading to the monastery can guarantee a very successful monastic life with God. If this spirituality is maintained, it develops and grows providing the monk the needed power and wisdom to overcome the ego and the various stumbling blocks which might face him in the monastery. Thus we can say that the experience of abandoning the world and the decision to become a monk are the basic foundations of his future experiences with God. If the monk preserves this deep in his heart and with all his heart, mind and will, and struggles to fulfil his promise before God, then he will sing with the Psalmist; "So I will sing praise to Your name forever, that I may daily perform my vows." (Psalm 61:8).

The Exodus from the World is a Measure of the Stature and Fullness of Christ

After Baptism and becoming filled with the Holy Spirit, we found that Jesus Christ continued to go the wilderness alone in retreat, fasting and praying. It is clear that he did not isolate Himself to get spiritually filled but to teach us that spiritual retreat is a basic requirement for attaining the stature of the fullness of Christ. In the same way baptism, crucifixion and resurrection are also requirements. In fasting the Holy forty days, Christ attained for humanity a certain stature of spirit, which is essential for every human being.

4. The Journey of the Monk to the Wilderness

In the forty days, Jesus Christ abandoned the world for the sake of the world, isolated Himself from people for the sake of people and departed from the disciples for the sake of the disciples. In His divine person, Jesus isolated humanity from the world which misled it. He took it out of its dusty nature, to live with it, with the Father in the wilderness, away from the lust of desire. In this blessed communion with the Father in solitude, He handed to humanity the means of overcoming the devil.

If a monk leaves the world, and succeeds in his way, he has risen above the worldly lust and is solely desiring God. Also, to leave his family, relatives and friends behind is an indication that he has conquered himself, which means that he is capable of loving and gathering the whole of humanity in his spirit and presenting it to God.

REACHING THE WILDERNESS

After the Lord ordered the children of Israel to leave the land of Egypt; "Then the children of Israel journeyed from Raamses to Succoth, about six hundred thousands men on foot, besides children." (Exodus 12:37), and "So God led the people around by way of the wilderness of the Red Sea. And the children of Israel went up in orderly ranks out of the land of Egypt." (Exodus 13:18), then "So they took their journey from Succoth and camped in Etham at the edge of the wilderness. And the Lord went before them by day in a pillar of cloud to lead the way, and by night in a pillar of fire to give them light, so as to go by day and night." (Exodus 13:20-21). When Pharaoh drew near to fight and bring them back to Egypt; "the children of Israel lifted their eyes, and behold, the Egyptians marched after them. So they were very afraid, and the children of Israel cried out to the Lord. Then they said to Moses, 'Because there were no graves in Egypt, have you taken us away to die in the wilderness? Why have you so dealt with us, to bring us up out of Egypt? Is this not the word that we told you in Egypt, saying, 'Let us alone that we may serve the Egyptians?' For it would have been better for us to serve the Egyptians than that we should die in the wilderness.' And Moses said to the people, 'Do not be afraid. Stand still, and see the salvation of the Lord, which He will accomplish for you today. For the Egyptians whom you see today, you shall see no more forever. The Lord will fight for you, and you shall hold your peace." (Exodus 14:10-14). Then the Lord ordered Moses to strike the Red Sea with his rod; "Then Moses stretched his hand over the sea; and the Lord caused the sea to go back by a strong east wind all that night, and made the sea dry into land, and the waters were divided. So the children of Israel went into the midst of the sea on the dry ground, and the waters were a wall to them on their right hand and on their left." (Exodus 14:21-22). They kept walking till they reached Sinai safely, while Pharaoh and his chariots drowned. When the Lord ordered Moses to strike the sea again; "Then the waters returned and covered the chariots, the horsemen, and all the army of Pharaoh that came into the sea after them. Not so much as one of them remained." (Exodus 14:28).

It is the same with the monk leaving the world. He spends the final days in the world but his mind is already in the wilderness. He wishes he could fly to the monastery and he exists in a strange spiritual pleasure with the grace of God carrying him on His arms till he reaches the monastery. Satan, the Pharaoh of the mind, never ceases to fight and goes after the monk with his soldiers and chariots, full of fears and doubts about the difficult journey and the long way. The devil at times appears to the monk entering the wilderness in the shape of an old, experienced and respected elder, reminding him of his family whom he has left behind grieving. Satan tells the person that there were saints who lived in the world and were married and had children yet they reached perfection, like Abraham, Isaac, Jacob, David and the others. So the person asks for God's support and the angels come and fill him with faith and confidence. At times angels appear in the form of a person to accompany the monk till he reaches the monastery.

Many thoughts may come to the person who is insisting on becoming a monk. For example:

- 'If they refuse to accept me in the monastery I'll stay by the monastery door till the Lord might soften their hearts and let me in'. This is what St. John the Short did when he stayed standing by the door of St. Bemwa's (Abba Pambo) cell for a whole week till the elder let him in.

- 'If they refuse to ordain me as a monk, I will live in the monastery as a servant for the monks to obtain their blessings and that is sufficient for me'.

He continues to think and pray and once he reaches the door of the monastery, he rejoices in unutterable joy, as though he has reached the gates of heaven. Then the bell rings in the monastery, as is the custom if a stranger comes, the monk responsible as a doorkeeper would come and let him in who then informs the Abbot, who then comes and talks to him. The new monk bows in a metania before the Abbot, asking in humility to accept him as his spiritual son and for his prayers and the prayers of the fathers. This day is a very special day in the life of a monk and he loves to remember it every now and then. St. Arsenius always reminded himself saying; "Arsani, meditate on the reason you left the world and came to the wilderness." God himself never forgets that day, so He keeps reminding the monk and strengthening him; "Go and cry in the hearing of Jerusalem, saying, 'Thus says the Lord: I remember you, the kindness of your youth, the love of your betrothal. When you went after me in the wilderness, in a land not sown." (Jeremiah 2:2). God also urges the monk to remember that day, lest he becomes puffed up and lose track of his target; "It is a night of solemn observance to the Lord for bringing them out of the land of Egypt. This is that night of the Lord, a solemn observance for all the children of Israel throughout their generations." (Exodus 12:42), also "It shall be as a sign on your hand and as frontlets between your eyes, for by strength of hand, the Lord brought us out of Egypt." (Exodus 13:16).

St. John Climacus said; "Leaving the world is a chosen hatred for every possession. Those who became monks, because of their many sins, they left the world behind, seeking the kingdom of God and His Love. If they do not reach any of this, then they have left the world in vain and they must struggle hard to obtain the reward. He who has left the world should break the bondage of his sins resembling those going to visit the cemetery where their beloved ones are buried. He should not stop sighing and weeping silently until he sees the Lord Christ coming, rolling the stone of inclemency from his heart, releasing his mind from death, ordering the angels to untie the bonds of his sins and let them go in peace."

Like those who left Egypt flying from the slavery of Pharaoh, the person seeking monasticism needs someone like Moses as an intercessor between them and God (the spiritual guide or confession father) to help them cross the sea of sin, or a guide like the angel who delivered Lot from Sodom. We should not go back, in our hearts, to Egypt, lest we perish or look behind at what we have fled from, like Lot's wife who was turned into a pillar of salt.

St. Macarius the Great said; "Let's flee, my brethren, from the world, as we escape from a serpent, because if a serpent bites someone, he can hardly survive. If we want to be real monks, we have to escape the world. It is much better for us to fight one war only, instead of many wars."

5. The Great Test

In the Wilderness

"Now it was told the king of Egypt that the people had fled, and the heart of Pharaoh and his servants was turned against the people; and they said, 'why have we done this, that we have let Israel go from serving us?' So he made ready his chariot and took his people with him. Also, he took six hundred choice chariots, and all the chariots of Egypt with captains over every one of them. And the Lord hardened the heart of Pharaoh king of Egypt, and he pursued the children of Israel; and the children of Israel went out with boldness. So the Egyptians pursued them, all the horses and chariots of Pharaoh, his horsemen and his army, and overtook them camping by the sea beside Pi Hahiroth, before Baal Zephon." (Exodus 14:5-9).

Pharaoh followed the children of Israel in order to take them back to serve him and to have authority over them once again. If the monk is going to the monastery, leaving behind some problems or disagreements with his family, the mental Pharaoh, (the devil) will follow him to the monastery, his family will continue to visit him and tempt him to return to them. The Abbot would explain to them that they had offered a living sacrifice to the Lord in giving Him their son, however, if they insist on talking to their son, he cannot prevent them.

This is the greatest test for the monk when facing his family. Does he have the strong will, or will he yield and return to them? Here, there are two types of monks, some prefer not to meet their families at all, lest they should have a strong influence on them through soft words and tears, while some monks continue to pray in their cells, asking the rest to also pray for them, and then they go to meet the family, and God gives them according to His great mercy and grace, to discuss matters and convince the family. There are also many types of families. Some are pious and they rejoice for their son in being a monk, while some become angry and furious and try and make him change his mind, while some continue to visit their son.

The Father of Confession and Obedience

The Abbot of the monastery then chooses an old and experienced monk to become the father of confession and spiritual guide to the novice monk, teaching and guiding him in his spiritual struggle, the life in the monastery, dealing with other monks and so forth. He must love his new son, and teach him how to fast, pray, do metanias and inform him about the tricks of the devil. He should open his heart to him expecting any questions or problems facing the new monk and accept him at any time. He must resemble St. Paul the great guide who says; "how I kept back nothing that was helpful, but proclaimed it to you, and taught you publicly from house to house, testifying to Jews, and also to Greeks, repentance toward God and faith toward our Lord Jesus Christ." (Acts 20:20-21).

On the other hand, the monk must obey his father of confession's guidance and commandments strictly in order to have everyone's love and blessing. He must also obey the Abbot, the Supreme Intendent, obeying his spiritual guide concerning prayers, fasting, number of metanias, reading the Holy Bible and other spiritual books. In this way, he can be sure that he is progressing moderately, not falling into the temptations of the devil by being lazy and reluctant or by going into extremes in terms of fasting and praying in excess of his bodily abilities. The early fathers considered the virtue of obedience in monasticism as one of the main cornerstones, along with celibacy.

There are many sayings concerning this virtue:

"Never do anything before consulting the Abbot of the monastery." St Anthony

"Beasts will yield to you if you are humble and obedient." St Anthony

"Do not be disobedient, lest you become a dwelling place for all evil things. Always put in your heart obedience to your father; thus you will have the blessing of the Lord." St Anthony

"A youth monk should consult the elders before doing anything, because I have seen many monks, after a great deal of toil, fall because they started depending on their own knowledge." St Anthony

"Obedience is the pride of a monk. God listens to an obedient monk, he can stand before the Crucified, the Lord of Glory, in intimacy because Jesus was crucified for us because of His obedience to the Father." St Irais

"A disciple will never reach the city of Peace unless he leaves his personal desires behind and obeys." St. Barsanufius

"A monk who obeys his father once and disobeys him once, is like a person who is building and demolishing, so all his toil is in vain." St. John Climacus.

"There is no salvation without guidance, and humility comes out of obedience, and we can become healed from all our pains through humility. 'Who remembered us in our lowly state; For His mercy endures forever.' (Psalm 136:5)." St. John Climacus.

Moses the Prophet is a wonderful example of a great guide, he was the spiritual guide and father to the children of Israel during their journey in the wilderness. Those who obeyed him were saved and reached the Promised Land, but those who murmured and yearned to return to Egypt died in the desert. They died spiritually and physically like Korah and Dathan, for whom the ground was split and swallowed them when they rebelled against Moses. Likewise for the person who wants to live in the wilderness as a monk, seeking to reach the Promised Land, the Heavenly Jerusalem, he must be obedient to his fathers and guides in the monastery.

"Joshua and Caleb were the only two to enter the Promised Land, out of 600 000 men because of their obedience to Moses according to God's orders. Those who are obedient will have calmness and peace while sitting in their cells in the monastery. Being obedient and having peace will kill the evil thoughts that attack a monk. He can thus cross the Jordan and enter the Promised Land, which is purity. My brethren, eradicate all the worldly thoughts that entered with you into the monastery." St. Felixinus about obedience.

Work in the Monastery

A novice monk is not left to sit all day in his cell for prayers and meditations but instead he is given jobs to do in the monastery. For example, he may have to assist in the kitchen most of the day, just leaving him some time for his prayers, metanias, readings and sleep, so that he does not become overwhelmed with thoughts about the world which he recently left.

The wisdom of this organisation for a novice - There are some spiritual benefits for giving the novice unpleasant and tiring jobs, no matter what his job and position was in the world, some of the benefits are:

1. **Teaching humility or growth in humility;** In the world he used to be served, not to serve and if he did any service to someone, he received many thanks and honours for this service. But in the monastery, he serves others in love and humility, even if he is serving someone who is lower than him in education and position. They might even be poor workers whom he cooks for, serves their meals, collects the plates and left overs, cleans the tables and wipes the floor etc., all of which he never performed when he was in the world. He may also serve the elders, if there is an opportunity, in order to obtain their blessings, according to St. Anthony's commandment; "Let everyone bless you", also as St. Paul says; "For we have great joy and consolation in your love, because the hearts of the saints have been refreshed by you, brother." (Philemon 7). Therefore, he who wants to learn humility should perform humble tasks.

2. **Teaching Tolerance;** At times a monk may face problems from those whom he serves. He must tolerate this and try to make everyone happy because he is the servant and they are his masters.

3. **Teaching Obedience;** He has to learn to obey his guide or whoever is older than him in the monastery, in addition to obeying the Abbot of the monastery and following his instructions.

4. **Teaching the virtue of love and hosting the strangers;** A novice doing any job in the monastery has a great opportunity to learn the virtue of cheerful love and giving to others. There are lots of poor workers working in the monastery to whom he can give some of his food, clothes and money. In this way, he is saving a treasure for himself in heaven, where no thief approaches or moth destroys.

5. The Great Test

5. **Teaching Organised Life;** The work a monk does, as well as his prayers in his cell and in the Church, are forming an organised and successful system for his life. In his cell he practices fasting, prayer, meditation, repentance etc., while during work he uses his time and energy in something beneficial for himself and the monastery lest the devil attack him with worldly thoughts, desires and lust.

At the beginning of his monasticism, St Anthony suffered a lot from thoughts, spending so many hours in his cell without any handwork. When he started complaining to God saying: "O Lord, I want to be saved, yet the thoughts are annoying me, what should I do?" The Lord sent him an angel dressed in, what we now know as monk's clothes, who prayed for a while, then braided some palm leaves and so on, then he said to him; "Anthony, do this and you will find rest." Since then, St Anthony made the uniform for monasticism and followed the instructions of the angel for praying and working and received rest with the grace and power of the Lord Jesus, glory be to Him.

Fathers' Sayings concerning the importance of work for a monk

"Choose to tire your body, together with prayers, fasting and watchfulness because this leads to chastity of heart, which then brings forth fruits of the soul." St Anthony

"The fear of God will dwell in your heart if you work by your hands." St Anthony

"The most important way to gain virtues is to tire the body (with knowledge and discernment) but laziness and reluctance brings fights from the devil." St Moses the Black

"Tire your body lest you should be disdained before the saints on the Judgment Day." St Moses the Black

"Do not love rest, as long as you are living." St Moses the Black

"Beware of futility lest you should be disgraced. You do better to work in order to feed the poor." St Moses the Black

"On top of all virtues comes a person who despises rest. He who looks after his body will experience troubles/tribulations which he will regret in his old age." St. Isaac the Syrian

"Our spiritual fathers made handwork as a canon; they considered it as one of the virtues for the following reasons:

- It relieves the monk from boredom,
- It is a means for a monk to earn his living and give to the poor,
- It prevents evil thoughts resulting from futility." One of the fathers

Joshua's victory over Amalek resembles a monk's victory over the devil. The story illustrates the importance of prayers and work to overcome the devil and his fights. Israel defeated Amalek by Moses' prayers till sunset on the mountain and by the effort of Joshua and the army fighting against the enemy. A person who wants to win in his struggle should never stop praying and working, leaving no opportunity for the enemy to attack him.

"The first virtue that a monk should have is humility which leads to obedience, which is one of the fruits of the Holy Spirit. From them all the other virtues will follow." St Felixinus

"St Paul says that our Lord Jesus Christ humbled Himself and obeyed the Father till death on the cross. Death entered into the world because of Adam's disobedience and sin followed. Likewise obedience brings all the spiritual joy and peace to whoever acquires it." St Felixinus

"Obedience is the daughter of humility which is the attitude of the monks in the monastery, in order to obey the spiritual father." St Felixinus

"As Joshua and Caleb obeyed Moses, they out of 600 000 men deserved to enter into the Promised Land. Those who didn't obey perished in the wilderness." St Felixinus

THE WARS FACING THE NOVICE

The wars which usually face the novice are; disputes, fulfilling the desires, disobedience, laziness, talking nonsense, lying, over caring for the bodily needs, negligence, having an envious eye, oversleeping. The worst of them is laughing, telling jokes, over eating and the wars of adultery which if submitted to will dim the brightness of the soul. All these wars can be defeated through the power and support of God in addition to obeying the spiritual father.

6. The Journey of the Monk to the Wilderness

The children of Israel used to say; "But the Lord hardened Pharaoh's heart, and he would not let them go", (Exodus 10:27), before departing the land of Egypt. Then after their exodus and crossing the Red Sea, God started teaching them different ways of worship and its rites, in order to worship Him according to His will. By worshipping God properly and not practicing any other contrary worship, they would not bring God's wrath upon them. He gave them the Law written with His Holy finger; He showed them the Tabernacle in order to follow its design and He ordered them how to offer sacrifices for thanksgiving or for their iniquities.

1. The Law

The Law occupies many chapters in the Book of Exodus. The Lord emphasised keeping, memorising and always following the Law; "And these words which I command you today shall be in your heart; you shall teach them diligently to your children, and shall talk of them when you sit in your house, when you walk by the way, when you lie down, and when you rise up. You shall bind them as a sign on your hand, and they shall be as frontlets between your eyes. You shall write them on the doorposts of your house and on your gates" (Deuteronomy 6:6-9), as the Law organises our relationship with God and man.

- The Law is the word of God, written with His Finger (Exodus 31:18), keeping it preserves us from sin and stumbling blocks during our journey in the wilderness of life. "Your word is a lamp to my feet and a light to my path." (Psalm 119:105).

- It is the pleasure of the souls; "But his delight is in the law of the Lord and in His law he meditates day and night." (Psalm 1:2). "And I will delight myself in Your commandments, which I love" (Psalm 119:47); and "Oh, I love your law! It is my meditation all the day." (Psalm 119:97).

- It gives knowledge and wisdom to whoever learns it; "I understand more than the ancients, because I keep Your precepts." (Psalm 119:100).

- It purifies one's heart and gives us life "You are already clean because of the word which I have spoken to you." (John 15:3); "It is the Spirit who gives life; the flesh profits nothing. The words that I speak to you are spirit, and they are life." (John 6:63).

After settling down in the wilderness, the spiritual father sets a system for the novice to follow in reading the Holy Bible, from both Testaments, as the Bible is very important in a monk's life, in his prayers and meditations. It is his daily spiritual meal with different parts from the Old and the New Testament. Reading the Holy Bible daily helps the monk to get in contact with God and allows the monk to get closer to God. If the person reads the Bible from his heart in awe, with prayers and in humility, he will definitely hear God's voice, receive guidance and be inspired. Besides the Holy Bible other spiritual books are recommended by the spiritual father, like the lives of the Fathers and their sayings.

There is a famous phrase of St Isaac; "the lives of the saints are so sweet to the ears of the humble, they are like water for new plants". Also; "he who neglects reading the Holy Bible and the spiritual books would never be ashamed when he sins".

St Anthony says: "Tire yourself in reading the Holy Books, for they will deliver you from impurity" and "Read the Holy Bible and spiritual books, thus God's mercy will come upon you quickly". Also "In your cell always do these things; read the books, plead to God and do some handwork."

2. The Tabernacle

God ordered Moses to collect different donations from the children of Israel in order to build the Tabernacle for worship. The Tabernacle is the house of God in the middle of Israel's tents; "And let them make Me a sanctuary, that I may dwell among them. According to all that I show you, that is, the pattern of the tabernacle and the pattern of all its furnishings, just so you shall make it." (Exodus 25:8-9). Moses made the Tabernacle exactly as God showed him on the mountain. It was in the shape of the Cross because the salvation of the Cross was in the Father's plan ever since the beginning. The tabernacle, with all its belongings was a sign of the Divine Incarnation, i.e. the dwelling of God amongst mankind.

There are many houses for God in the desert where monks live. The monastery is generally called God's house because it is built in the desert where no one else could live except them. They worship God totally devoting their lives to spiritual worship. There is more than one church in any monastery and these are usually beautiful old churches which give the worshippers a spirit of prayer and the feeling of God's presence, as Jacob felt long ago when he said; "How awesome is this place! This is none other than the house of God, and this is the gate of heaven." (Genesis 28:17).

Usually these churches are lit with candles or lanterns, they are so quiet having no sounds of transportation or any sort of noise, so prayers take place in total serenity giving an opportunity for the senses and mind to be released with God.

The fathers always ask the novice monk to attend all the prayers in the church in order to learn and practice being in the house of God, as David said; "How lovely is Your tabernacle O Lord of Hosts! My soul longs, yes, even faints for the courts of the Lord; my heart and my flesh cry out for the living God…For a day in Your courts is better than a thousand. I would rather be a doorkeeper in the house of my God than dwell in the tents of wickedness." (Psalm 84:1-2, 10).

"If the church bell rings, do not be reluctant to go." St Anthony

"Stand in the church as if you are standing in heaven." Another father

The individual worship is performed in the monks cell (room), which is built and designed in a way to encourage the monks spiritual life. The cell consists of two rooms. The inner room is called the 'prison' because the monk imprisons himself willingly to carry out the different personal worships such as prayers, metania, reading, writing, sleeping etc.. St Isaac said; "he who loves God will love sitting in his prison and his cell". The outer room is for cooking, sitting with other monks, if for any reason they want to talk to him, etc.

3. THE SACRIFICES

There were two altars in the Tabernacle:

1. **The Altar of Burnt Offering**, located at the entrance of the Tabernacle, where the sacrifices were burnt because it was forbidden to go into the Tabernacle and meet God without offering sacrifices and reconciling with God. "You shall make an altar of acacia wood, five cubits long and five cubits broad – the altar shall be square and its height shall be three cubits. You shall make its horns on its four corners; its horns shall be of one piece with it. And you shall overlay it with bronze. Also you shall make its pans to receive its ashes, and its shovels and its basins and its forks and its fire pans; you shall make all its utensils of bronze. You shall make a grate for it, a network of bronze; and on the network you shall make four bronze rings at its four corners. You shall put it under the rim of the altar beneath, that the network may be midway up the altar. And you shall make poles for the altar, poles of acacia wood, and overlay them with bronze. The poles shall be put in the rings, and the poles shall be on the two sides of the altar to bear it. You shall make it hollow with boards; as it was shown you on the mountain, so shall they make it." (Exodus 27:1-8).

2. **The Altar of Incense**; "You shall make an altar to burn incense on; you shall make it of acacia wood. A cubit shall be its length and a cubit its width – it shall be square – and two cubits shall be its height. Its horns shall be of one piece with it. And you shall overlay its top, its sides all around, and its horns with pure gold; and you shall make for it a molding of gold all around. Two gold rings you shall make for it, under the molding on both its sides. You shall place them on its two sides, and they will be holders for the poles with which to bear it. You shall make the poles of acacia wood, and overlay them with gold. And you shall put it before the veil that is before the ark of the Testimony, before the mercy seat that is over the Testimony where I will meet with you. Aaron shall burn on it sweet incense every

morning; when he tends the lamps, he shall burn incense on it. And when Aaron lights the lamps at twilight, he shall burn incense on it, a perpetual incense before the Lord throughout your generations." (Exodus 30:1-8).

On these two altars people in the wilderness offered their worship to God and all the different sacrifices; the Burnt Offering (Leviticus 1), the Grain Offering (Leviticus 2), the Peace Offering (Leviticus 7), the Sin Offering (Leviticus 5) and the Trespass Offering (Leviticus 5). That was to offer thanksgiving and repentance to the mighty God who miraculously delivered them from the land of Egypt. Leaving the world, choosing monasticism and living in the wilderness is a great sacrifice, where a person offers himself totally to God, no partner to share this sacrifice, no wife, children, family, only God. This is representative of what happened to the burnt offering; "He shall kill the bull before the Lord; and the priests, Aaron's sons, shall bring the blood and sprinkle the blood all around on the altar that is by the door of the tabernacle of meeting. And he shall skin the burnt offering and cut it into its pieces. The sons of Aaron the priest shall put fire on the altar and lay the wood in order on the fire. Then the priests, Aaron's sons, shall lay the parts, the head, and the fat in order on the wood that is on the fire upon the altar but he shall wash its entrails and its legs with water. And the priest shall burn all on the altar as a burnt sacrifice, an offering made by fire, a sweet aroma to the Lord." (Leviticus 5:1-9). It was all consumed for the Lord, no one, not even the priest or the person who offered it was to take any of it for himself.

The person who lives in the desert as a monk offers to God many other daily sacrifices in the monastery. The first of these is the sacrifice of prayer and praise which are; "the fruit of our lips, giving thanks to His name (Hebrews 13:15") ; "For we will offer the sacrifices of our lips. (Hosea 14:2)". Prayer is the most important work of a monk living in the desert. It is a great work, worthy of the monk devoting his life to it until he reaches the highest levels in the life of prayer.

The Agpia is the daily canon of prayers for a novice monk, he prays it twice, once alone in his cell and once at church with the rest of the monks. He is also given a canon of metanias, a number set by his father in confession, that is appropriate to his health and spiritual level. A novice has to attend the Liturgies held in the monastery, partaking of the Holy Communion, in order to gain power to help him against the fights of the body and the devil.

The monk offers to God:

- The sacrifice of lifting up one's arms; "Let my prayer be set before You as incense, the lifting up of my hands as the evening sacrifice." (Psalm 141:2); "Unto You I lift up my eyes, O You who dwell in the heavens." (Psalm 123:1); and "I will lift up my eyes to the hills from whence comes my help? My help comes from the Lord who made heaven and earth." (Psalm 121:1,2).

- The sacrifice of lifting up one's soul; "To You, O Lord, I lift up my soul. Let me not be ashamed; let not my enemies triumph over me. Indeed, let no one who waits on You be ashamed; let those be ashamed who deal treacherously without cause." (Psalm 25:1-3).

- The sacrifice of fasting and asceticism; "I beseech you therefore brethren, by the mercies of God, that you present your bodies a living sacrifice, holy, acceptable to God, which is your reasonable service." (Romans 12:1).

- The sacrifice of celibacy and chastity, as a sweet aroma to the Lord.

- The sacrifice of obedience, "For you do not desire sacrifice, or else I would give it; You do not delight in burnt offering. The sacrifices of God are a broken spirit, a broken and a contrite heart. These, O God, You will not despise" (Psalm 51:17-18).

- The sacrifice of alms giving, "But do not forget to do good and to share, for with such sacrifices God is well pleased." (Hebrews 13:16).

Thus a novice lives an angelic life in the monastery, living in heaven while he is still on earth; "that your days and the days of your children may be multiplied in the land of which the Lord swore to your fathers to give them, like the days of the heavens above the earth." (Deuteronomy 11:21). The wilderness will then be turned into heaven, through their prayers and sacrifices. Isaiah the Prophet says; "The foolish person will no longer be called generous, nor the miser said to be bountiful; for the foolish person will speak foolishness, and his heart will work iniquity to practice ungodliness, to utter error against the Lord, to keep the hungry unsatisfied, and he will cause the drink of the thirsty to fail. Also the schemes of the schemer are evil; he devises wicked plans to destroy the poor with lying words, even when the needy speak justice. But a generous man devises generous things and by generosity he shall stand." (Isaiah 32:5-8); "the wilderness and the wasteland shall be glad for them, and the desert shall rejoice and blossom as the rose. It shall blossom abundantly and rejoice, even with joy and singing. The glory of Lebanon shall be given to it the excellence of Carmel and Sharon. They shall see the glory of the Lord, the excellency of our God." (Isaiah 35:1,2).

7. The Rite of Ordaining Monks for Monasticism

When the Lord saw Joshua's obedience to his teacher Moses, his love to people, his holy zeal towards God's commandments, God ordered Moses to ordain Joshua to be his successor in leading the children of Israel and said; "Take Joshua the son of Nun with you, a man in whom is the Spirit, and lay your hand on him; set him before Eleazar the priest and before all the congregation, and inaugurate him in their sight. And you shall give some of your authority to him that all the congregation of the children of Israel may be obedient. He shall stand before Eleazar the priest, who shall inquire before the Lord for him by the judgment of the Urim; at his word they shall go out, and at his word they shall come in, both he and all the children of Israel with him, all the congregation." So Moses did as the Lord commanded him. He took Joshua and set him before Eleazar the priest and before the entire congregation. And he laid his hands on him and inaugurated him, just as the Lord commanded by the hand of Moses." (Numbers 27:18-23).

So it is with the novice monk, he spends a few months under training, to be observed by his confession father regarding his obedience and humility, how he deals with others, whether he is active or lazy etc.. This is also a chance for the novice to test himself whether he is serious in his intentions for monasticism or not. If the Abbot finds no complaints whatsoever about this novice monk and everyone has a good report of him, especially his confession father, then he is ready to be ordained.

After the Agpia prayers in the Vespers, the Abbot opens the curtain of the sanctuary, the candles are lit on the altar and the monk's clothes are placed thereon. The monk stands before the sanctuary door, the Abbot asks; "Does anyone have any objections for ordaining brother… as a monk"? If no one objects, the Abbot gives the monk some advice, then the monk bows in a metania in front of the Sanctuary door, then in front of the monasterys' door as a sign of his obedience to the rules, then in front of his brethren the monks, then he asks absolution and forgiveness from everyone. He then brings his clothes from the altar; he carries one end and the Abbot carries the other end, then the Abbot signs them 3 times with the cross while saying his new name as a monk. The monk kisses the Abbot's hand, takes the clothes and puts them on any saint's relics present in the church, then puts them on while the deacons chant a suitable hymn. The Vesper prayers are continued as normal, and then all the monks come and congratulate the new monk, wishing him to abide and grow in grace, to be a blessing for the monastery and the whole wilderness generally.

The spiritual father comes and takes his confession and prays the absolution, which is very important before the ordination that takes place the next morning so as to ensure that he is starting his new life pure and clean of any sin or iniquity, as St Anthony says; "Monasticism is like baptism concerning starting a new life. The Spirit that descends in the Holy Baptism comes also during ordination. It purifies the monk." St Anthony witnessed this personally, as he says; "I saw my soul coming out of my body, the devil tried to hamper it in the air and judge it, but I heard a voice from heaven saying "I've forgiven everything for him since his childhood till he became a monk, his sins are forgiven through his monasticism."

The monk stays awake at the church till the morning, together with other monks surrounding him happily. They talk about the struggle of monastic life, the life of great saints, especially the saint of his namesake (i.e. his monastic name).

They pray the Midnight Prayer the Midnight Praise and raising Morning Incense. The Abbot then comes to continue the rite of Ordination, which are prayed before the bodies of the saints present in the church in order that the spirit of these saints may come upon the newly ordained monk and support

7. The Rite of Ordaining Monks for Monasticism

him in his struggle. This is what Moses did with the seventy elders of the tribe of Israel, as God ordered him; "Gather to Me seventy men of the elders of Israel, whom you know to be the elders of the people and officers over them; bring them to the tabernacle of meeting, that they may stand there with you. Then I will come down and talk with you there. I will take of the Spirit that is upon you and will put the same upon them; and they shall bear the burden of the people with you, that you may not bear it yourself alone." (Numbers 11:16-17); "So Moses went out and told the people the words of the Lord, and he gathered the seventy men of the elders of the people and placed them around the tabernacle. Then the Lord came down in the cloud, and spoke to him, and took of the Spirit that was upon him, and placed the same upon the seventy elders; and it happened, when the Spirit rested upon them, that they prophesied, although they never did so again." (Numbers 11:24-25).

THE RITE OF ORDINATION

The monk lies on his back before the relics of the saints, putting both hands on his chest like a dead person in a coffin because monasticism is death to the world. The readings are very similar to those of a funeral service with its sad tunes.

The Abbot prays the thanksgiving prayer, then the incense procession and then the prophecies as follows:

- From the Book of Genesis (Genesis 12:1-7), which exhorts on abandoning the world, obeying God's voice and seeking the land of Canaan like Abraham.

- From the book of Deuteronomy (Deuteronomy 8:1-9), which exhorts one to keep and follow the Commandments in order to be worthy to enter Canaan, the Promised Land.

- From Joshua son of Sirach (Chapter 2:1-5) which exhorts on tolerating temptations and clinging to the Lord, in order to reach eternal life safely.

Then the Litany of the Sick is prayed; "Come, you children, listen to me; I will teach you the fear of the Lord. Who is the man who desires life, and loves many days, that he may see go? Keep your tongue from evil, and your lips from speaking guile. Depart from evil, and do good; Seek peace, and pursue it." (Psalm 34:11-15); "I have done justice and righteousness; do not leave me to my oppressors. Be surety for Your servant for good; Do not let the proud oppress me. My eyes fail from seeking Your salvation and Your righteous word. Deal with Your servant according to Your mercy, and teach me Your statutes. I am Your servant; Give me understanding, that I may know Your testimonies. It is time for You to act, O Lord, For they have regarded Your law as void. Therefore I love Your commandments More than gold! Therefore all Your precepts concerning all things I consider to be right; I hate every false way." (Psalm 119:21-28); "My heart is severely pained within me, and the terrors of death have fallen upon me. Fearfulness and trembling have come upon me, and honor has overwhelmed me. And I said, "Oh, that I had wings like a dove! For then I would fly away and be at rest. Indeed, I would wander far off, and remain in the wilderness. I would hasten my escape from the windy storm and tempest." (Psalm 55:4-8).

The Pauline is read in Coptic in the sad tune, then read in Arabic from Ephesians 6:10-20; "Finally, my brethren, be strong in the Lord and in the power of His might. Put on the whole armour of God, that you may be able to stand against the wiles of the devil. For we do not wrestle against flesh and blood, but against principalities, against powers, against the rulers of the darkness of this age, against spiritual hosts of wickedness in the heavenly places. Therefore take up the whole armour of God, that you may be able to withstand in the evil day, and having done all, to stand. Stand therefore, having girded your waist with truth, having put on the breastplate of righteousness, and having shod your feet with the preparation of the gospel of peace; above all, taking the shield of faith with which you will be able to quench all the fiery darts of the wicked one. And take the helmet of salvation, and the sword of the Spirit, which is the word of God; praying always with all prayer and supplication in the spirit, being watchful to this end with all perseverance and supplication for all the saints, and for me, that utterance may be given to me, that I may open my mouth boldly to make known the mystery of the gospel, for which I am an ambassador in chains, that in it I may speak boldly, as I ought to speak."

The Trisagion is sung in the sad tune, then the Litany of The Gospel, the Psalm and Gospel in Coptic, are sung in the Pascha tune. The Psalm is read in Arabic; "In You, O Lord, I put my trust; let me never be ashamed; Deliver me in Your righteousness. Bow down Your ear to me, deliver me speedily; be my rock of refuge, a fortress of defense to save me." (Psalm 31:1-2), then the Gospel; "When He had called the people to Himself, with His disciples also, He said to them, 'Whoever desires to come after Me, let him deny himself, and take up his cross, and follow Me.'" (Mark 8:34).

7. The Rite of Ordaining Monks for Monasticism

An exposition is read by the Abbot where he asks God to accept the prayers, the fasting, repentance and confession of the new monk, to give him a pure heart, wisdom and an alert mind. Then the Three Great Litanies, the Creed and the Litany of the Reposed is prayed. A prayer is said by the Abbot asking God to give the new monk blessings so as to help him escape the desires and overcome the tricks of the evil spirits.

The monk then stands up for the Abbot to cut his hair 5 times in the shape of the cross, saying the five signings, as a Nazarite used to do; "Then the Nazarite shall shave his consecrated head at the door of the tabernacle of the meeting, and shall take the hair from his consecrated head and put it on the fire which is under the sacrifice of the peace offering." (Numbers 6:18).

The Abbot prays, signs the clothes, then clothes the monk while saying; "Put on the garment of righteousness and the shield of light and bear fruits worthy of repentance through Christ." He puts on the Qalansewa (hood) and says; "Put on the hood of humility and the helmet of salvation, do good deeds through Christ". He puts on the girdle and says; "Gird yourself with all the bindings of God and the power of repentance through Christ".

These rites are done in imitation of Moses when consecrating Aaron and his children to serve the Lord; "And Aaron and his sons you shall bring to the door of the tabernacle of meeting, and you shall wash them with water. Then you shall take the garments, put the tunic on Aaron, and the robe of the ephod, the ephod, and the breastplate, and gird him with the intricately woven band of the ephod. You shall put the turban on his head, and put the holy crown on the turban. And you shall take the anointing oil, pour it on his head, and anoint him. Then you shall bring his sons and put tunics on them. And you shall gird them with sashes, Aaron and his sons, and put the hats on them. The priesthood shall be theirs for a perpetual statute. So you shall consecrate Aaron and his sons." (Exodus 29:4-9).

Then he reads the absolution, takes the monk by the hand before the altar, reading the monastic law written in the book, a part of which says; "You should know the amount of grace you have acquired because you have become in the image of angels, you are now a soldier for Christ, ready for a good struggle. You are now renewed from the world's evil deeds; so, keep yourself pure to become a good soldier for Christ, the King of kings and resist the wars of Satan and his evil soldiers. Keep your covenant to worship God in awe and reverence, pray the Psalms, with vigils at night, pray the Psalmody and church prayers, do all this with moderate fasting. Listen to him who guides you to

God's path and His Holy Commandments till death, in order to gain the crown of the children of God and inherit the Kingdom of Heaven."

The monk attends the Holy Liturgy, partakes of the Holy Communion, then goes in a procession while the bells of the monastery ring declaring the joy of everyone.

An Exposition to be said Celebrating the Ordination of a New Monk

"Rejoice with us today my fathers and brethren, for our honourable monk (…..) who put on the angelic robe and was granted the good talents, which the Lord gives to whoever He desires and pours His Holy Spirit on those who please Him. Our great father St Anthony the father of all monks said: "I saw the Holy Spirit which descends in Baptism, descending on him who is ordained as a monk".

St Paul says in Romans 9:16; "It is not of him who wills, nor of him who runs, but of God Who shows mercy." Also St James said in James 1:17-18; "Every good gift and every perfect gift is from above, and comes down from the Father of lights, with whom there is no variation or shadow of turning. Of His own will He brought us forth by the word of truth, that we might be a kind of first fruits of His creatures."

*Our Lord Jesus declared the path of perfection to the rich youth, Jesus said to him; "If you want to be perfect, go, sell what you have and give to the poor, and you will have treasure in heaven; and come, follow Me." (Matthew 19:21).

Let's glorify the Lord and thank Him for His rich blessings and ask Him to give us understanding to open our mouths today and rejoice for the honour given to the monk (….).

Blessed are you, the pure monk, for gaining this honourable gift, which our master Christ, glory be to Him, has granted you. When you put on the holy garb of monasticism the heavenly and earthly cried out, "Axios, Axios.. We ask our Lord, God and Saviour Jesus Christ to preserve your monasticism in purity and righteousness and complete your struggle following the path of the saints, in order to rejoice with them in the heavenly Jerusalem and hear that rejoicing voice from the divine mouth saying, "enter into the joy of Your Lord" (Matthew 25:23). Through the intercessions of the pure St Mary, the father of all monks St Anthony and all the saints. Amen.

Pope Shenouda during the ordination of a group of monks at St Bishoy's monastery. The monks habits are placed on the relics of Saint Bishoy on the top right. and the ordained monks are lying under the Altar curtains in front of the altar and next to the relics of St Bishoy.

8. A Day in a Monk's Life

How does a monk spend his day?

Many people ask this question especially:

1. The novice monks who are eager in spirit and want to live their monastic life in honesty.
2. The youth who is thinking of becoming a monk, in order to see if they are capable of coping with this life or not. Personally before joining the monastery, I used to read lots of books dealing with monasticism and the first chapter I looked for was talking about how a monk spends his day, whether in the monastery or inside his cell.
3. Those who edit books about monasticism.
4. Common people because there are still lots of mysteries about monastic life that people do not know.

Prophet Jeremiah says; "Thus says the Lord: stand in the ways and see, and ask for the old paths, where the good way is, and walk in it; then you will find rest for your souls. But they said, 'We will not walk in it.'" (Jeremiah 6:16). So, if we follow the old paths, definitely we will reach the heavenly Kingdom because these are ready paved paths.

Some of the elder fathers' sayings:

"The monks have to follow this order in their daily life: From 3pm they do whatever the superintendent asks them to do, in obedience and submission, as taught by St Paul, 'Do all things without complaining and disputing.' A monk should fear the threatening as St Paul states; 'nor complain, as some of them also complained, and were destroyed by the destroyer'". St Paphnutius

"Read some Psalms, memorise some, and do some readings so you can spend the day pleasing God. Our early fathers didn't follow a timetable for prayers, they used to spend the day between reading, praying the Psalms, working their hand work." St Barsanuphius

"In your cell, spend some time reading the Psalmody, some time in praying the Psalms, some time in testing your thoughts. Do not fix a limit for the Psalmody or prayers from the heart, but practice them as much as God might give you. Never neglect reading and inner prayers. Do a bit of everything of the above mentioned in your day." St Barsanuphius

"Our elderly fathers did all in God's fear as St Paul taught in his epistles. If you are sitting in your cell remember your sins, weep and ask the Lord's forgiveness. If your mind goes astray, bring it back quickly." St Barsanuphius

"In the morning wash your hands and bow in a metania in front of the cross, in order to concentrate your thoughts and gets your heart inflamed with God's love. Weep and plead to the Lord. Pray this short prayer before reading the Holy Bible, 'O Lord, make me worthy to enjoy the Mysteries of Your Only Begotten Son. Shine unto my heart with Your pure light. Grant me Your grace, do not let the mention of Your Holy Name depart from my heart day and night.' Preferably read the Book of Acts and St Paul's Epistle in order to cleanse yourself till 9am. Then stand before the cross, do a metania, pray the 3rd hour prayer, do not hasten in praying the Psalms, feel the words you are reading and meditate on them. Then read the elders book till the 6th hour. After the 6th hour prayer, keep working while doing metanias." St Felixinus

Our fathers consider the handwork done in their cell, in God's fear, equivalent to gaining one of the virtues, for two reasons;

i) it relieves you from boredom, as St Anthony was taught by the angel

ii) the monk earns his food and living needs from selling his handwork and he is also able to give alms.

From the 9th hour till evening he eats, prays and does metanias. At night, raise your heart to God thankfully, for all His grace and mercy during the day. Do this in great fear and awe because the night sacrifice is the most acceptable to God, as David says; "Let my prayer be set before You as incense, the lifting up of my hands as the evening sacrifice." (Psalm. 141:2). Then eat moderately and do not indulge in many kinds of food, do not fill your stomach lest the enemies attack you at night. Finish your canon after eating, as directed by the elder fathers. Spend the night in three parts; Psalms with metanias, reading and singing praises, in order to receive the comfort of the Holy Spirit throughout the whole night. A monk who spends the night in vigil resembles the angels of light who are always glorifying the Lord. Be keen to complete the seven Agpia prayers set by our elderly fathers because they preserve our life.

As St Nilus of Sinai says, "Split the day into some work, some prayers and some readings. Keep your mind meditating and contemplating."

*Also as spoken by St Isaiah of Scetis, "Pray a lot during the night, because prayer is the light to soul. Spend around two hours of prayers and singing Psalms at night before sleeping. Do not be reluctant in the Agpia prayers lest you fall in the hands of your enemies, the Psalms preserve you from the sin of impurity. Eat once daily, moderately and stay awake at night also moderately. Spend half of the night in prayers and the other half to have a rest. If you are living in a cell, fix an amount of food and certain time to eat regularly because the destruction of the soul comes from the greedy stomach. In the morning, read God's word first, before starting any work, then do whatever you have to do in your cell actively. In your cell do these 3 things: i) Hard work, ii) Pray and read, iii) Always think that today is your last day alive and so you will not sin".

The author of "Studies in the History of Egyptian Monasticism" (page 153), records how the monks were keen to pray the seven prayers of the Agpia. They pray the Sunset Prayer and before sleeping prayer then have a little rest at the first quarter of night, then whoever had slept wakes up for the midnight prayer, which they consider very important quoting David the Prophet's words; "At midnight I will rise to give thanks to You" (Psalm 119:62). He who is reluctant to rise for prayer is considered reluctant in giving thanks and gratitude to God. At dawn they pray the Morning Prayer after which they are not allowed to sleep but rather spend around three hours reading the Holy Bible and meditating. The Morning Prayers, the third hour prayer at 9am, the 6th hour prayer at 12pm and the 9th at 3pm.

The author of "The Coptic Monasticism at the time of Anba Macarius" (Page 362) says; "The day of the monks starts immediately after Midnight, with the Prayer and praise of Midnight, then they keep reading the Holy Bible till sunrise, following the first great commandment of St Anthony, 'Pray always, memorise the Psalms and the Holy Bible before sleeping and straight after waking'. By doing this a monk is not giving any chance for evil thoughts to come through his mind."

The early fathers used to read the Holy Bible or Psalms while doing their handwork because weaving baskets was an easy job that did not require much attention, thus they mastered memorising huge parts of the Holy Bible.

Handwork - Handwork ends by 12 noon, then a monk has some rest, each according to his needs.

Lunch and the period of abstaining from food - The early fathers fixed 3pm to be the hour for the only meal eaten by a monk. This time was set by devout fathers having deep spiritual experience. A novice was not to eat before or after this fixed time.

The Ninth hour prayer - Palladius recorded that at 3pm (the 9th hour prayer) you could hear the Psalmody praises clearly everywhere in the desert of Egypt. John Cassian also approved of this fact. Thus the 9th hour prayer was prayed by all monks before they ate their only meal.

Sleeping - A monk might sleep after Sunset prayer up till Midnight prayer, then he wakes up and starts his prayers.

The Importance of the Cell - According to one of the fathers, the cell resembles the fiery furnace of the Three Young Saints at the time of Daniel the Prophet, when they were talking to the Lord and praising Him from amidst the fire (they were enjoying His presence with them). So amidst the fire of struggle, the dew of grace and the Holy Spirit refreshes the monk.

The cell is not a place to rest and relax, but it is a place of pain, struggle, joy and crying out to God. It is a place where God comes and visits us. The cell is a sign of a ascetic life and renouncing the world, it is a sign of continuous resurrection to God. It is written; "Now it came to pass, while he blessed them, that he was parted from them and carried up into heaven." (Luke 24:51). So isolating ourselves from people allows us to ascend to heaven and go up step by step in virtues.

A monk's continuous aim is; "but let it be the hidden person of the

8. A Day in a Monk's Life

heart, with the incorruptible ornament of a gentle and quiet spirit, which is very precious in the sight of God." (1 Peter 3, 4), as the Psalmist says; "The royal daughter is all glorious within the palace; Her clothing is woven with gold. She shall be brought to the King in robes of many colors; the virgins, her companions who follow her, shall be brought to You." (Psalm 45:13-14). The life of the cell and the life of the communion in the monastery are like wings for the monk, if he uses them in harmony, they will lift him up quickly towards holiness.

Once, a monk went to St Moses the Black and asked him a word of benefit, so the elder said to him; "go back to your cell and the cell will teach you everything." The same advice was given by Anba Arsenius to a monk, the monk followed the advice for three days then started feeling bored, so he weaved some palm leaves, then he felt hungry, so he ate a little, then prayed for a while, then read the Holy Bible and so on. So with the grace of God he kept doing this till he calmed down and had authority over himself and defeated the thoughts fighting him.

MONASTICISM IN THE EARLY AGES

The day used to start at midnight, Cassian fixed this at the crow of the rooster (around 12am). The monks used to wake up as if repeating with St Paul; "You are all sons of light and sons of the day. We are not of the night nor of darkness but let us watch and be sober." (1 Thessalonians 5: 5-6).

The Apostle Paul fulfilled these words practically while he was imprisoned with Silas, their feet fastened in stocks; "But at midnight Paul and Silas were praying and singing hymns to God, and the prisoners were listening to them."(Acts 16:25), and as a result of this strong prayer; "Suddenly there was a great earthquake, so that the foundations of the prison were shaken; and immediately all the doors were opened and everyone's chains were loosed." (Acts 26:26).

The monk starts his day with the Midnight Prayer as the Psalmist says; "At midnight I will rise to give thanks to You, because of Your righteous judgment" (Psalm 119:62); then the Morning Prayer, which finishes around 6am, then he does his metanias in humility, reads the Holy bible from both Old and New Testaments and does his handwork inside his cell till 12pm.

St Paul teaches a very important commandment; "that you also aspire to lead a quiet life, to mind your own business, and to work with your own hands, as we commanded you, that you may walk properly toward those who are outside, and that you may lack nothing. (1 Thessalonians 4:11-12).

The third and sixth hour prayers fall during this time, so he can pray them in his cell, while doing his handwork. But if he can't concentrate, he might stop and pray. During work, he can memorise short prayers like, "My Lord Jesus Christ have mercy on me, a sinner". He can then have a rest, each according to his need.

A lovely story is mentioned in The Paradise of The Holy Fathers about the great St John the Short; "An elder monk came to St John the Short and found him asleep. He saw an angel standing by St John waving cool air on him to relieve him from the heat and so he left. When St John awoke, he asked his disciple if there was an elder here, then he knew that this elder was a righteous one and that he saw the angel."

After the rest, the monk starts preparing his meal. Then he prays the ninth hour prayer at 3pm followed by eating his food. He then reads the lives of the fathers and spiritual books, if he needs any guidance he can go to his teacher. At sunset, around 5pm he prays the sunset and the prayer before sleeping. He then keeps praying until he falls asleep. He sleeps for few hours, then he wakes up for midnight prayers starting a new day by the grace of God. Nowadays there is no fixed system for a monk's day, but he rather organises his day by agreement with his confession father.

Here roughly is a order for a monk's day in the monastery:

- Around 4am he wakes up, goes to church for the midnight prayer with the other monks, then the Midnight praise, followed by the Holy Liturgy. He can either attend the Liturgy if it is his turn to serve, or go back to his cell and pray his own prayers.

- He prays the first, third and sixth hour prayers, followed by metanias, then reads the Holy Bible.

- Around 9am the work starts in the monastery, whether in the church, bookshop, stores, guests room, bakery, garden, etc..

- Usually, the novice carry out the more tiring jobs because they are not yet used to spend long periods in their cell. The sick and elders are exempted from any jobs.

- A monk should recite Psalms and prayers during his work, he can

8. A Day in a Monk's Life

also pray some of his hourly prayers, for example the sixth and ninth hour.

- He then eats at the time that his confession father had fixed for him and then has a rest, but if he had already slept in the morning, he shouldn't rest again.

- He then prays the ninth, sunset and before sleeping prayers, followed by some readings until the church bell rings, upon which he goes to the church for prayers with all the monks.

- Reading is appropriate in summer during daytime, but in winter when the nights are longer, he does all his readings, writings, mediations, cleaning his cell etc..

- Then he can have some time to visit other sick monks or walk in the desert and mediate, he can pray the Veil prayers and part or all of the midnight prayer, or he can learn some hymns, tunes or the Coptic language.

- He goes back to his cell for dinner and finishes the rest of his prayers.

- He goes to bed around 10pm in order to wake at 4am. Some monks live in separate cells or caves outside the monastery in the desert or mountains. They have their own special system of spending their day. This is a endowment given to us, let us use it appropriately and please the Lord in all our deeds.

9. The Life of Solitude in Monasticism

Solitude is a high level of monasticism which a monk reaches after first living in a monastery with other monks in a communal system. The Coptic/Greek work "monachos" which is translated "monk" means "a person living in solitude", illustrating that the aim of monasticism is to live in complete solitude.

Sometimes the monk locks himself in his cell for days or weeks, seeking to live totally with God. He might leave the monastery with the permission of his spiritual father to live in a cave in the mountain, coming back to the monastery at intervals. He progresses in his life, abstaining from food and staying in vigil for longer times and his soul and heart also increases in their purity and serenity.

The Fruits of Solitude and Serenity

A monk who lives in solitude will become free from the bonds on the soul and will gain many virtues such as peace, humility, love, meekness, comfort… etc.. Then he will be worthy of the Divine Mercy and the unity of his mind with God.

Conditions of Solitude and Serenity

1. **Fasting and Meditation** - Fasting purifies the mind and body. It makes the person capable of continuous prayer.

2. **Concentration** - Concentration in controlling our senses and thoughts and ignoring all outer distractions such as blaming others or pre-occupying ourselves with the world. The continual mention of the name of our Lord Jesus Christ within our hearts will keep us safe from going astray.

3. **Closing the Three Doors** - St Isaac says: "If we close these three doors, we will find Christ dwelling inside; the door of the cell, the door of the senses and the door of our heart."

The following are some examples from the lives of the saints.

1. **The Great St Anthony Father of the Monks** - St Athanasius the Apostolic mentions that St Anthony lived in complete solitude, never seeing the face of a man for 30 years. During these years he experienced the fruits of quietness; he emptied his mind from the worries of the world, its news and its trifle matters so he may only be filled with God.

2. **St Macarius the Great** - He dug a tunnel from his cell half a mile in length and dug another cell at the end of the tunnel so whenever people came to him, he went secretly to the other cell through the tunnel.

3. **St Arsenius the teacher of the Kings' children** - He used to live in a cell 32 miles away from the monastery. He had a stone in his mouth for 3 years in order to practice silence. He is famous for the saying; "Many times I have spoken and regretted, but I never regretted being silent."

4. **St Isaac the Syrian** - A great recluse that spent the last years of his life in the desert of Scetis. He wrote a book about the rite of solitude in monasticism, which is one of the most wonderful books written on this topic.

10. Monasticism and the Holy Bible

Although the word monk or monasticism is not mentioned clearly in the Holy Bible because monasticism was not widely known as it is today, yet there are many heroes in the Holy Bible who offered all their lives as a living acceptable sacrifice on the altar of worship. They loved prayer and turned it into a way of life. They also loved calmness and serenity, living in celibacy and purity and all these virtues are the basis of monasticism.

The Old Testament

Elijah The Prophet lived in celibacy and voluntary poverty being fed by the ravens and a poor widow. Elijah loved the mountains, where he used to live in communion with God. He used to go to the city according to God's order to carry out a mission.

When Ahaz the King was sick; "Then the king sent to him a captain of fifty with his fifty men. So he went up to him, and there he was sitting on the top of a hill. And he spoke to him: Man of God, the king has said, come down!" (2 Kings 1:9) and finally, after pleading three times to Elijah, "And the angel of the Lord said to Elijah, Go down with him; do not be afraid of him. So he arose and went down with him to the king." (2 Kings 1:15). Even when Jezebel threatened to kill him, Elijah fled to the wilderness, "And there he went into a cave, and spent the night in that place; and behold, the word of the Lord came to him, and He said to him "What are you doing here, Elijah?" (1 Kings 19:9), and there, the Lord appeared to him in the still small voice and asked him to carry out important work.

Elijah looked like a ascetic recluse when the messengers of Ahaz the King described him; "So they answered him, 'He was a hairy man, and wore a leather belt around his waist,' and he said, 'It is Elijah the Tishbite.'" (2 Kings 1:8). The king immediately knew it was Elijah.

Elijah was a man of prayer and worship, having a very strong relationship with God, when he offered the sacrifice on Mount Carmel, he cried to the Lord saying; "Hear me, O Lord, hear me, that this people may know that You are the Lord God and that You have turned their hearts back to You again. Then the fire of the Lord fell and consumed the burnt sacrifice, and the wood and the stones and the dust, and it licked up the water that was in the trench." (1 Kings 18: 37-38), then "Now it happened in the meantime that the sky became black with clouds and wind, and there was a heavy rain. " (1 Kings 18:45).

Through Elijah's prayers fire came down from heaven and consumed the two captains of fifties with their fifties (2 Kings 1). As he had great favour in the eyes of the Lord, the widow's son came back to life; "Then the Lord heard the voice of Elijah and the soul of the child came back to him and he revived. And Elijah took the child and brought him down from the upper room into the house, and gave him to his mother. And Elijah said, 'See your son lives.'" (1 Kings 17:22-24).

Elisha The Prophet followed his teacher Elijah's footsteps in asceticism:

- He was a celibate.

- He loved the life of the mountains like his teacher. Especially Mount Carmel, where people used to come and meet him (2 Kings 4: 25). He only visited the city to carry a message, as a prophet and teacher for the people.

- He never owned anything, once the sons of the prophets came to him, so he sent his disciple to gather some herbs from the field to cook for them (2 Kings 4: 38-41).

- He was poor and people used to give him alms; "Then a man came from Baal Shalisha, and brought the man of God bread of the first fruits, twenty loaves of barley bread, and newly ripened grain in his knapsack. And he said, 'Give it to the people, that they may eat', and his servant said, 'What shall I set this before one hundred men?' He said again, 'Give it to the people, that they may eat'; for thus says the Lord, 'they shall eat and have some left over.' So he set it before them, and they ate and had some left over, according to the word of the Lord." (2Kings 4:42-44).

- Many miracles were performed through his prayers, such as healing the bitter water (2 Kings 2:21-22), increasing the widow's oil (2 Kings 4:1-7), raising the Shunammite's son (2 Kings 4:20-37), healing Naaman from leprosy (2 Kings 5:14) and many other miracles that God used to perform through the prayers of His beloved Elisha.

Jeremiah the Prophet was ornamented with lots of beautiful monastic characteristics.

- He was a celibate, according to a Divine order; "The word of the Lord also came to me saying: "You shall not take a wife, nor shall you have sons or daughters in this place." (Jeremiah 16:1-2).

- He also loved to live in the wilderness and if he did not have the chance to go there, he said; "Oh, that I had in the wilderness a lodging place for wayfaring men; that I might leave my people, and go from them!" (Jeremiah 9:2). As David the Prophet says; "Indeed I would wander far off, and remain in the wilderness. I would hasten my escape from the windy storm and tempest." (Psalm 55:7-8). The "windy storm and tempest", are the troubles and tribulations of the world that may cause us to forget our eternity.

- Jeremiah was a humble, quiet, repentant person; "It is good for a man to bear the yoke in his youth. Let him sit alone and keep silent because God has laid it on him; Let him put his mouth in the dust. There may yet be hope. Let him give his cheek to the one who strikes him, and be full of reproach. For the Lord will not cast off forever though he causes grief, yet He will show compassion according to the multitude of His mercies. For He does not afflict willingly nor grieve the children of men." (Lamentations 3:27-33). "Let us lift our hearts and hands to God in heaven. We have transgressed and rebelled; You have not pardoned." (Lamentations 3:41-42).

- He was a man of prayers and tears; "Oh that my head were waters and my eyes a fountain of tears, that I might weep day and night for the slain of the daughter of my people!"(Jeremiah 9:1). He always prayed to God (Jeremiah 32:16) and the Lord always used to talk to him.

The New Testament

The Pure Virgin St Mary, the quiet beautiful pure dove, her parents took her to the temple at the age of three, where she remained in prayer and fasting, serving the holies in meekness. She was fed by the angels and gave her food to the poor (from the Kiahk Psalmody).

We notice from the Annunciation icon that she was praying when the angel appeared and said; "Rejoice, highly favoured one, the Lord with you; blessed are you among women." (Luke 1:28). The praise that she said at Zechariah's house is proof of her life of prayer and worship. She was a perpetual virgin even after the miraculous birth of our Saviour Jesus Christ.

Anna the Prophetess, the daughter of Phanuel, was another star in the sky of worship and consecration; "and this woman was a widow of about eighty four years, who did not depart from the temple, but served God with fasting and prayers night and day." (Luke 2:37). She deserved to be a prophetess and to see Baby Jesus.

Mary, the sister of Lazarus, was a vivid example of the life of worship and quietness. She used to sit at the feet of Jesus listening to His sweet touching words. David the Psalmist describes such people; "Surely the righteous shall give thanks to Your name; the upright shall dwell in Your presence."(Psalm 140:13).

This life style is highly appreciated by Lord Jesus, when Martha complained to Jesus; "Lord, do You not care that my sister has left me to serve alone? Therefore tell her to help me. And Jesus answered and said to her, 'Martha, Martha, you are worried and troubled about many things. But one thing is needed, and Mary has chosen that good part, which will not be taken away from her.'" (Luke 10:40-42). The 'good part' means the contemplation because all other works and practices will cease at the departure of a our lives but we will never be deprived of contemplation, prayer and praises to God, which will continue with us in eternity and by which we will participate with the angels and saints.

John the Baptist, the greatest born of women, the courageous in truth, who lived in pure celibacy all the days of his life. He was brought up in the wilderness; "So the child grew and became strong in spirit, and was in the deserts till the day of his manifestation to Israel." (Luke 1:80). He lived in complete ascetism even in regards to his clothes and food, under the guidance of the Greatest Teacher.

Monastic Characteristics mentioned in the Holy Bible

Celibacy- There are many verses in the Holy Bible that encourage and praise celibacy:

"Do not let the son of the foreigner who has joined himself to the Lord speak, saying: The Lord has utterly separated me from His people. Nor let the eunuch say, here I am, a dry tree." For thus says the Lord; "To the eunuchs who keep My Sabbaths and choose what pleases Me, and hold fast My covenant, even to them I will give in My House and within My walls a place and a name better than that of sons and daughters; I will give them an everlasting name that shall not be cut off." (Isaiah 56:3-5)

"Now concerning the things of which you wrote to me: it is good for a man not to touch a woman." (1 Corinthians 7:1). "But I say to the unmarried and to the widows: it is good for them if they remain even as I am." (1 Corinthians 7:8). "But I want you to be without care. He who is unmarried cares for the things that belong to the Lord how he may please the Lord. But he who is married cares about the things of the world how he may please his wife. There is a difference between a wife and a virgin. The unmarried woman cares about the things of the Lord, that she may be holy both in body and in spirit. But she who is married cares about the things of the world how she may please her husband."(1 Corinthians 7: 32-34).

"Then I looked, and behold, a Lamb standing on Mount Zion, and with Him one hundred and forty-four thousand, having His Father's name written on their foreheads. And I heard a voice from heaven, like the voice of many waters, and like the voice of loud thunder. And I heard the sound of harpists playing their harps. And they sang as it were a new song before the throne, before the four living creatures, and the elders; and no one could learn that song except the hundred and forty-four thousand who were redeemed from the earth. There are the ones who were not defiled with women, for they are virgins. These are the ones who follow the Lamb wherever he goes. These were redeemed from among men being first fruits to God and to the Lamb. And in their mouth was found no guile for they are without fault before the throne of God." (Revelations 14:1-5).

Prayer - As for prayer, which is the main job of a monk, Isaiah the Prophet tells us that man is created to offer prayers and praises to our Lord, exactly like the angels, thus he can be happy and live according to their heavenly life; "Everyone who is called by My name, Whom I have created for My glory; I have formed him, yes, I have made him." (Isaiah 43:7); also "The Lord is well pleased for His righteousness' sake; He will magnify the law and make it honourable." (Isaiah 43:21).

Our Lord Jesus was a great example to follow in prayers. He used to go to the mountain and spend the night in prayers. He advises us to pray at all times, waiting for the coming of the Lord; "Take heed, watch and pray; for you do not know when the time is." (Mark 13: 33).

Dispossession (Voluntary Poverty) - Dispossession or voluntary poverty is one of the bases of monasticism. Jesus lived poor, having nowhere to lay down His head. When he wanted to pay taxes; "Nevertheless, lest we offend them, go to the sea, cast in a hook, and take the fish that comes up first. And when you have opened its mouth, you will find a piece of money; take that and give it to them for Me and you." (Matthew 17:27). He also renounced positions and fame; "Then when Jesus perceived that they were about to come and take Him by force to make Him king, He departed again to a mountain by Himself alone." (John 6:15).

Jesus is calling everyone to this simple life style; "No one can serve two masters, for either he will hate the one and love the other, or else he will be loyal to the one and despise the other. You cannot serve God and mammon." (Matthew 6:24). His disciple John the Beloved also says; "Do not love the world or the things in the world. If anyone loves the world, the love of the Father is not in him. For all that is in the world – the lust of the flesh, the lust of the eyes, and the pride of life – is not of the Father but is of the world." (1 John 2:15-16).

The disciples also lived in poverty like their Master. St Paul says; "as sorrowful, yet always rejoicing; as poor, yet making many rich; as having nothing, and yet possessing all things." (2 Corinthians 6:10).

Obedience - Obedience is one of the cornerstones of monasticism. Our Lord Jesus said; "My food is to do the will of Him who sent Me, and to finish His work." (John 4:34). Also; "For I have come down from heaven not do My own will, but the will of Him who sent me." (John 6:38); and "I speak what I have seen with My Father, and you do what you have seen with your father. They answered and said to Him: Abraham is our father. Jesus said to them, If you were Abraham's children, you would do the works of Abraham." (John 8: 38-39).

The Lord is asking us to enter through the narrow door of obedience, because it is a sure and safe way; "Enter by the narrow gate; for wide is the gate and broad is the way that leads to destruction, and there are many who go in by it. Because narrow is the gate and difficult is the way which lead to life, and there are few who find it." (Matthew 7:13-14).

St Paul also says; "Obey those who rule over you, and be submissive, for they watch out for your souls, as those who must give account. Let them do so with joy and not with grief, for that would be unprofitable for you." (Hebrews 13:17). That is obeying Christ's commandments, the confession father and spiritual guide.

Dying to the world - This is the objective of a monk, about which St Paul says; "This is a faithful saying: for if we died with Him we shall also live with Him. If we endure, we shall also reign with Him. If we deny Him, He also will deny us." (1 Timothy 2:11-12). "If then you were raised with Christ, seek those things which are above, where Christ is, sitting at the right hand of God. Set your mind on things above, not on things on the earth. For you died and your life is hidden with Christ in God." (Colossians 3:1-3).

Other Monastic Virtues - The Psalmist says; "But it is good for me to draw near to God; I have put my trust in the Lord God, that I may declare all Your works." (Psalm 73:28).

The monastic life, with its continuous mention of the Name of the Lord and living in solitude away from the noise of the world, will aid a monk to cling to the Lord all the times. The Lord addresses this soul by saying; "I remember you, the kindness of your youth, the love of your betrothal, when you went after Me in the wilderness, in a land that was not sown." (Jeremiah 2:2). "Therefore I will return and take away My grain in its time and My new wine in its season, and will take back My wool and My linen, given to cover her nakedness." "I will betroth you to Me forever; yes I will betroth you to Me in righteousness and mercy; I will betroth you to Me in faithfulness, and you shall know the Lord." (Hosea 2: 9, 20).

Solomon the Wise says; "A fool also multiplies words. No man knows what is to be; who can tell him what will be after him?" (Ecclesiastes 10:14). Also; "For thus says the Lord God, the Holy One of Israel: In returning and rest you shall be saved; in quietness and confidence shall be your strength." (Isaiah 30:15); also; "I have set watchmen on your walk, O Jerusalem, who shall never hold their peace day or night. You who make mention of the Lord do not keep silent, and give Him no rest till He establishes and till he makes Jerusalem a praise in the earth." (Isaiah 62: 6-7). "Then he spoke a parable to them, that men always ought to pray and not to lose heart." (Luke18: 1). "Pray without ceasing" (1 Thessalonians 5:17). "For this reason we also thank God without ceasing, because when you received the word of God which you heard from us, you welcomed it not as the word of men, but as it is in truth, the word of God, which also effectively works in you who believe." (1 Thessalonians 2:13).

All these verses are applied to the monk who enjoys the serenity of the wilderness, lifting his heart to the Lord at all times in praises and prayer.

The church needs the servants and priests to guide and protect their children in the evil world, yet it also needs the monks who are worshipping and praying all day to support the servants in the world. They are the rear guard of the army or the unseen protectors of the church.

Monasticism is Based on Verses from the Holy Bible

It is mentioned in the life of St Anthony the Great, the father of the monks, that on his way to church he was contemplating on our Lord Jesus' invitation to His disciples to follow Him. Upon entering the church he heard the Gospel reading of the day in which Jesus says; "If you want to be perfect, go sell what you have and give to the poor, and you will have treasure in heaven and come follow Me." (Matthew 19:21). Immediately after he left the church, he gave all his possessions to the poor (around 300 acres of best quality land), only keeping a small portion for his sister. But when he entered the church again, he heard; "Therefore do not worry about tomorrow, for tomorrow will worry about its own things. Sufficient for the day is its own trouble." (Matthew 6:34), so he also gave the rest to the poor, took his sister to a house for ladies and then headed to the wilderness. He always advised his children; "Any deed that you do, should be supported by a verse from the Holy Bible."

Saints Maximos and Domadius

11. Monasticism is a Continuation of the Era of Martyrdom

Monasticism started at the end of the 3rd century. Many of the early monks were living during the era of martyrdom. When these pioneer's found they had no share in receiving a crown of martyrdom, they devoted their lives to a voluntary, slow martyrdom. They chose to tolerate whatever they can in perseverance, fasting, prayers…etc. for the sake of their Christ who suffered and died for their salvation. Each of them has repeated with St. Paul; "that I may know Him and the power of His resurrection, and the fellowship of His sufferings, being conformed to His death." (Philippians 3:10). No one could know the power of the resurrection of our Lord unless he experiences His suffering and pains on the Cross.

St. Anthony and The Desire for Martyrdom

In the life of St Anthony we read that he yearned for martyrdom during the era of Maximianous the idolater king, so he went to Alexandria, yet king Maximianous didn't call him or kill him. The Lord preserved St Anthony from martyrdom for the benefit of monasticism. He was serving the confessors in jails and dungeons.

St Anthony and the monks who followed his path, offered their bodies to another kind of martyrdom; killing the desires of the body through strict asceticism and adhering to strict rules to follow in the desert. They considered monasticism as crucifying the body with its desires, to share with the Beloved Crucified Lord Jesus in His sufferings; "It is enough for a disciple that he be like his teacher, and a servant like his master. If they have called the master of the house Beelzebub, how much more will they call those of his household!" (Matthew 10:25). They repeated with St Paul; "I have been crucified with Christ; it is no longer I who live, but Christ lives in me; and the life which I now live in the flesh I live by faith in the Son of God, who loved me and gave Himself for me." (Galatians 2:20).

12. Monks are Faithful Soldiers to the Lord Jesus Christ

Those who live the life of monasticism are an army for the Lord Jesus. It is total consecration for His service through prayer, worship, fasting, longsuffering, fighting the devil...

Characteristics of the Faithful Soldier

A faithful soldier is always ready for war, courageous and prepared to fight in order to win or die in honour; "For to me, to live is Christ, and to die is gain" (Philippians 1:21). St Paul advices his disciple Timothy; "This charge I commit to you, son Timothy, according to the prophecies previously made concerning you, that by them you may wage the good warfare." (1 Timothy 1:18). Also St Paul said; "For to you it has been granted on behalf of Christ, not only to believe in Him, but also to suffer for His sake, having the same conflict which you saw in me and now hear is in me." (Philippians 1:29-30).

A faithful soldier is always watching at night, not pre-occupying himself with other affairs, lest the enemy come and attack him suddenly. St Paul says; "No one engaged in warfare, entangles himself with the affairs of this life, that he may please him who enlisted him as a soldier." (2 Timothy 2:4).

A good soldier learns the art of fighting in order to win as St Paul says; "And also if anyone competes in athletics, he is not crowned unless he competes according to the rules." (2 Timothy 2:5); "Let each one remain in the same calling in which he was called." (1 Corinthians 7:20), also St Peter says; "Therefore, brethren, be even more diligent to make your calling and election sure, for if you do these things you will never stumble; for so an entrance will be supplied to you abundantly into the everlasting kingdom of our Lord and Saviour Jesus Christ." (2 Peter 1:10-11).

The faithful soldier obeys his leaders even up till death, the same with the monk, obedience is one of the main characteristics of monasticism. The good soldier always trains himself for the tactics of war; "This being so, I myself always strive to have a conscience without offense toward God and men." (Acts 24:16); "Lead me in Your truth and teach me, for You are the God of my salvation; on You I wait all the day." (Psalm 25:5); "But solid food belongs to those who are of full age, that is, those who by reason of use have their senses exercised to discern both good and evil." (Hebrews 5:14). The spiritual wars with the devils have their own strategies and tactics gained from experience.

THE UNIFORM OF THE SOLDIER

The soldier wears a special uniform during the war, in order to be protected from the fatal shots of the enemy. The devil launches a great war with the monk who is wearing the uniform of monasticism, as he is a soldier in the army of Jesus Christ; "The wicked will see it and be grieved; He will gnash his teeth and melt away; the desire of the wicked shall perish."(Psalm 112:10). When Satan sees this angelic uniform, he remembers the great fathers who defeated him and becomes more furious.

THE STRENGTH OF THE UNIFORM OF THE MONKS

St Anthony the father of all monks wanted to test the power of a monk's uniform, so he got a dummy and clothed it in this uniform and saw the devils shooting arrows at it from afar. The saint then mocked this ridiculous behaviour and informed the devils that it was just a dummy, so the devils answered; "It is the clothes that are infuriating us."

The reason for the devils hatred of the uniform is that monks remind them of the holiness which they lost and because monks are recruited in the army of Lord Jesus, specialised in fighting the devils.

THE RITE OF MONASTICISM

A novice gets ready for ordination, first by filling his heart with the Divine sayings in order to be a faithful soldier in the army of Lord Jesus and by preparing to face the unseen war launched by Satan, as St Paul says; "Finally, my brethren, be strong in the Lord and in the power of His might. Put on the whole armour of God, that you may be able to stand against the wiles of the devil. For we do not wrestle against flesh and blood, but against principalities, against powers, against the rulers of the darkness of this age, against spiritual hosts of wickedness in the heavenly places. Therefore take up the whole armour of God, that you may be able to withstand in the evil day, and having done all, to stand. Stand therefore, having girded your waist with truth, having put on the breastplate of righteousness, and having shod your feet with the preparation of the gospel of peace; above all, taking the shield of faith with which you will be able to quench all the fiery darts of the wicked one. And take the helmet of salvation, and the sword of the Spirit, which is the word of God." (Ephesians 6:10-17).

After the prayers of ordination on the novice and the clothes, the abbot clothes the monk, while saying different prayers. While clothing him with the robe he says; "Put on the garment of righteousness and the shield of light, and bear fruits worthy of repentance through Jesus Christ our Lord, to whom worship, honour, and glory are due." While clothing him with the 'qalansewa' (cap) he says; "Put on the qalansewa of humility and the helmet of salvation and bear good fruits through Jesus Christ our Lord glory be to Him. Amen."

While clothing him with the girdle he says; "girdle your waist with the bindings of God and the power of repentance through Jesus Christ our Lord."

THE ANGEL GIVING ST ANTHONY THE CLOTHES OF MONASTICISM

This story is written in "The Paradise of The Holy Fathers"; "One day St Anthony was sitting in his cell, he felt bored and in low self-esteem, so he prayed to God asking for help, then he saw a man sitting before him wearing the clothes of monks plaiting some palm branches, then he stopped and stood up, prayed for a while, then plaited the branches etc.. This man was an angel of the Lord Whom He sent to comfort St Anthony saying to him, "Do this and you will find rest.""

THE CLOTHES OF A MONK AND THEIR SPIRITUAL MEANING

The Holy Eskeem - The 'Eskeem' is a Coptic word which means 'shape'; it is a length of plaited leather with crosses placed at equal distances. The eskeem surrounds the chest and the back. Two big crosses are in it, one for the chest and one for the back and there are 12 more smaller crosses.

The hermits who have reached high levels of spirituality wear it, living by the following strict practices and rules:

1. To read the 150 Psalms daily.
2. To pray the Midnight Praise daily.
3. To do 500 metania daily.
4. To be quiet, not exceeding 7 words daily.
5. To read a lot in the Holy Bible and the lives and sayings of the saints.
6. Fast daily till Sunset.
7. To eat, drink, and sleep minimum so that he reaches mental and psychological serenity and purity.

THE RITE OF WEARING THE ESKEEM

It is like the Rite of ordaining monks to a great extent, but the prayers and crossings are done here on the leather plaited Eskeem. In one of the prayers, the Abbot prays; "we ask and entreat to Your Goodness O Lover of mankind, make him worthy of this Eskeem, which is the sign of the Holy Cross of Your Only Son, and His life-giving death, to live with Him in eternal life forever. Amen." Then he clothes the monk with the Eskeem saying; "Put on the seal which is a token of the Kingdom of heaven, the holy Eskeem. Carry on your arms the sign of the glorified Cross. Follow our Saviour and Lord Jesus Christ, the True God, to inherit the Light of eternal life through the power of the Holy Trinity, the Father, the Son and the Holy Spirit." After finishing the prayers and reading the commandments, the monk participates in the Holy Liturgy and partakes of the Holy Communion.

THE CLOTHES OF A MONK

The robe and the qalansewa are made of black material, the girdle made of leather with three plaited leather crosses on it.

The Girdle in the Holy Bible - Many teachings were mentioned concerning the girdle. Lord Jesus advised His disciples; "Let your waste be girded and your lamps burning" (Luke 12:35), i.e. to be ready and watching all the time, like a soldier, so that whenever their master comes, He finds them ready; "And if he should come in the second watch, or come in the third watch, and find them so, blessed are those servants." (Luke 12:38). St Peter also advises us to wear the unseen girdle; "Therefore gird up the loins of your mind, be sober, and rest your hope fully upon the grace that is to be brought to you at the revelation of Jesus Christ." (1 Peter 1:13). In the life of the Apostles, the girdle meant asceticism and being free of possessions, as the Lord said to them; "Provide neither gold nor silver nor copper in your money belts," (Matthew 10:9). The girdle, which Aaron the Priest used to wear, was made of pure white cotton, symbolising purity (Leviticus 16:4).

The Qalansewa (Cap) - The qalansewa was originally a stripe of material 70cms or 80cms long and 7cms wide, with two crosses on both ends. The monk used to put it on his head under the cap, with the cross on top of the brain to preserve it from evil thoughts. It reached the girdle around the waist, forming the shape of a cross. But now, the qalansewa is a full cap covering the head and neck up till the shoulders only. It looks like a baby's hood, indicating the spirit of simplicity which should be in the monk. There are 12 crosses, 6 on both sides of a qalansewa denoting the 12 disciples. There are stitches along the middle of it, in remembrance of the incident when the devil snatched St Anthony's qalansewa while the saint kept hold of it until it was torn into two. The saint fixed the tear by stitching the two halves together.

13. Monasticism, Better Than a Kingdom

In our Christian history we hear about many saints who abandoned their worldly kingdom for the sake of the love of the true King Jesus Christ and His eternal Kingdom.

Some examples are; St Maximos and St Domadios, St Ilarion the daughter of King Zeinon who disguised herself in monk's clothes at the age of 28 and went to Scetis wilderness, St Anastasia, St Annasimon and many others.

Monasticism with its serenity and calmness, attracts many rich, educated and talented youth. They abandon their wealth, positions and important responsibilities in pursuit of the salvation of their souls.

A Good Example

We see in our Lord Jesus a good example of escaping from the vainglory of the world; "Therefore when Jesus perceived that they were about to come and take Him by force to make Him king, He departed again to a mountain by Himself alone." (John 6:15). This verse is the beginning of the Gospel reading in the Prayers of the Veil which is included in the Agbia especially for monks. This reading was chosen to remind the monks that they are following in the footsteps of their Beloved Lord, choosing the narrow door of monasticism, through which they'll reach their Master safely.

14. Monasticism, a Christian Philosophy

"There wouldn't be a nation better than Christians on earth if they follow the commandments and there wouldn't be Christians better than monks if they keep their rites and vows." An elder

"The true Christians are the best people and the monks are the best among Christians." Another elder

"Although we (the monks) are belittled by people, let us consider the honour we have before God." St John the Short

The Introduction of the Rites of Ordaining Monks

If someone wants to become a monk he has to spend 3 years learning the rules of monasticism. The novice is taught from the wisdom and lives of the monastic fathers taken from the book, "The Paradise of The Holy Fathers". He is also guided to the true philosophy of monasticism.

The Preface of the Coptic Monasticism Law

Monasticism is the philosophy of the Christian Law; the monks are heavenly human beings and earthly angels, following Christ to the best of their abilities, imitating His disciples in asceticism, forsaking possessions, rejecting the world and its desires and following Christ's commandments. They love

God more than their parents, children, wives and wealth. They are happy to toil on earth for the sake of eternal life.

From the above mentioned, we notice that monasticism is the philosophy of Christianity at a sublime spiritual level where the person recognises the vanity of this world and its glory.

When a monk seeks the Lord, follows His commandments, prays continuously and practices all the other spiritual means, he becomes filled with the wisdom of God because God is True Wisdom; "Christ, in whom are hidden all the treasures of wisdom and knowledge." (Colossians 2:2-3), who has said; "I, wisdom, dwell with prudence, and find out knowledge and discretion." (Proverbs 8:12). Job the righteous also says; "And to man he said, 'Behold, the fear of the Lord, that is wisdom, and to depart from evil is understanding.'" (Job 28:28); and David the Psalmist says; "The fear of the Lord is the beginning of wisdom; A good understanding have all those who do His commandments. His praise endures forever." (Psalm 111:10).

So the fear of the Lord is the beginning and the head of all wisdom because the Lord says; "A son honours his father, and a servant his master. If then I am the Father, Where is My honour? And if I am a Master, where is My reverence? Says the Lord of Hosts to you priests who despise My name, Yet you say, 'In what way have we despised Your name?'" (Malachi 1:6).

The monk fears the Lord as a son his Father, not as a slave his master. He offers God toil and weariness, humility and thanksgiving out of love, so that the fear of God is always mixed with loving God.

Thus, the monk becomes the greatest philosopher and the wisest wise man. Monasticism becomes the greatest philosophy and the holiest wisdom.

QUIETNESS LEADS TO DISCERNMENT AND WISDOM

The life of quietness, serenity, contemplation, reading the Holy Bible and the lives of saints etc., in a monk's life leads to wisdom, discernment and spiritual enlightenment and thus his life becomes pure according to Jesus Christs' words; "You are already clean, because of the word which I have spoken to you." (John 15:3), his soul becomes seasoned with grace; "Salt is good, but if the salt loses its flavour, how will you season it? Have salt in yourselves, and have peace with one another." (Mark 9:50), also; "Let your speech always be with grace, seasoned with salt, that you may know how you ought to answer each other." (Colossians 4:6). St Anthony praised the virtue of discernment, considering it the one that protects all other virtues.

Once a group of fathers gathered around St Anthony discussing the best virtue. Some said it is prayer and fasting, some said ascetism and others mercy. At the end, St Anthony concluded; "All the virtues that you mentioned my brethren are essential for those who seek the Lord, but we've seen many monks fasting, praying and living in solitude in the wilderness, yet they perished at the end because they didn't have the virtue of discernment".

DISCERNMENT IS THE EYE AND LIGHT OF THE SOUL

A monk learns discernment through his continuous communion with the Lord Jesus, reading the Holy Bible, the fathers' sayings and listening to his spiritual father's advice. Through these good works he can be confident that he is learning to discern between good and bad, the right path from the wrong path. Discernment teaches the monk and any person how to live moderately so that he is neither struck by the right temptation, (i.e. practicing ascetism more than he can tolerate and falling in vain glory), nor by the left temptation (which is being reluctant, lazy and having low self esteem).

As St Moses the Black says, "Three things lead to discernment:

1. Silence because it leads to ascetism
2. Ascetism because it lead to weeping and fear
3. Fear because it leads to humility and begins meditation on eternal life; this takes the monk to complete love and a soul which is totally free from any spiritual diseases. Then a person will know that he is close to God and he will then prepare for departure."

MONASTICISM AND MEDITATION IN THE UNLIMITED

A monk's job is to meditate on God, the Unseen and Unlimited, believing in the eternal life and trying to taste it on earth. The life of a monk is a pre-taste of eternity.

MONASTICISM SOLVES CONTRADICTIONS

Death and life are contradictory, yet a monk combines them in his life;

he dies to the world and its desires and he lives for God in a life of worship and contemplation.

The cross is composed of two pieces of wood crossing each other, i.e. we have to die here in the world in order to live in eternity and we must crucify ourselves on the cross, in order to live in Christ.

A monk combines between abandoning his family and relatives, while still loving them and praying for their salvation. A monk also combines between the deeds of mercy and the life of serenity and contemplation because while he is living in solitude, his heart is full of love to all the creation; he prays for the safety of the church and the world.

15. Monasticism is a Life of Repentance

When John the Baptist started his preaching, he cried out; "Repent, for the kingdom of heaven is at hand!" (Matthew 3:2). He said of his baptism; "I indeed baptize you with water unto repentance," (Matthew 3:11), the people that he baptised; " were baptized by him in the Jordan, confessing their sins" (Matthew 3:6). Repentance was also the preaching of our Lord Jesus; "Now after John was put in prison, Jesus came to Galilee, preaching the gospel of the kingdom of God, and saying, 'The time is fulfilled, and the kingdom of God is at hand. Repent, and believe in the gospel.'" (Mark 1:14-15). "But go and learn what this means: I desire mercy and not sacrifice. For I did not come to call the righteous, but sinners to repentance." (Matthew 9:13). Jesus told us how joyful the Kingdom of heaven would be for the repentance of one sinner; "I say to you that likewise there will be more joy in heaven over one sinner who repents than over ninety-nine just persons who need no repentance." (Luke 15:7). In His Divine Sermon on the Mountain, He pointed to repentance and described it as the narrow gate. He advised everyone to go through it; "Enter by the narrow gate; for wide is the gate and broad is the way that leads to destruction, and there are many who go in by it. Because narrow is the gate and difficult is the way which leads to life, and there are few who find it." (Matthew 7:13-14). Jesus knows that without repentance there is no salvation, even if we pray, fast, do charitable deeds or services, so He says; "I tell you, no;

but unless you repent you will all likewise perish" (Luke 13:3); again ; "I tell you, no; but unless you repent you will all likewise perish" (Luke 13:5).

Also, after His Resurrection, He said to His Apostles; "and that repentance and remission of sins should be preached in His name to all nations, beginning at Jerusalem" (Luke 24:47). St Paul also, talking to Agrippa preached; "Therefore, King Agrippa, I was not disobedient to the Heavenly vision, but declared first to those in Damascus and in Jerusalem, and throughout all the region of Judea, and then to the Gentiles, that they should repent, turn to God, and do works befitting repentance." (Acts 26:19-20); also; "Truly, these times of ignorance God overlooked, but now commands all men everywhere to repent" (Acts 17:30). In all his Epistles he kept encouraging people to repent; "Or do you despise the riches of His goodness, forbearance, and longsuffering, not knowing that the goodness of God leads you to repentance?" (Romans 2:4); "Therefore, leaving the discussion of the elementary principles of Christ, let us go on to perfection, not laying again the foundation of repentance from dead works and of faith toward God" (Hebrews 6:1). St Peter also advises; "Repent therefore and be converted, that your sins may be blotted out, so that times of refreshing may come from the presence of the Lord." (Acts 3:19).

BASICS AND MEANS OF SUCCESSFUL REPENTANCE

Avoiding stumbling blocks and sinful places - as St Paul said: "Flee from youthful lusts; but pursue righteousness, faith, love, peace with those who call on the Lord out of a pure heart." (2 Timothy 2:22). In the wilderness, a monk lives away from the places of sin and stumbling and as time passes by, he forgets all the worldly talk and scenes of which the righteous Lot suffered; "And many will follow their destructive ways, because of whom the way of truth will be blasphemed. By covetousness they will exploit you with deceptive words; for a long time their judgment has not been idle, and their destruction does not slumber. For if God did not spare the angels who sinned, but cast them down to hell and delivered them into chains of darkness, to be reserved for judgment; and did not spare the ancient world, but saved Noah, one of eight people, a preacher of righteousness, bringing in the flood on the world of the ungodly; and turning the cities of Sodom and Gomorrah into ashes, condemned them to destruction, making them an example to those who afterward would live ungodly; and delivered righteous Lot, who was oppressed with the filthy conduct of the wicked (for that righteous man, dwelling among them, tormented his righteous soul from day to day by seeing and hearing their lawless deeds)" (2 Peter 2:2-8). Thus the monk lives a life of holy struggling

15. Monasticism is a Life of Repentance

and having zeal for repentance to please God, in order to attain the life of purity and sweet communion with God; "Blessed are the pure in heart, for they shall see God" (Matthew 5:8).

Avoiding luxurious living - St Paul says: "But she who lives in pleasure is dead while she lives" (1 Timothy 5:6). God warns those who indulge in worldly desires and luxurious living, ignoring their eternal life; "Therefore hear this now, you who are given to pleasures, who dwell securely, who say in your heart, I am, and there is no one else besides me; I shall not sit as a widow, nor shall I know the loss of children; but these two things shall come to you in a moment, in one day: the loss of children, and widowhood. They shall come upon you in their fullness because of the multitude of your sorceries, for the great abundance of your enchantments." (Isaiah 47:8-11). In the wilderness, a monk lives a ascetic life in voluntary poverty, he only takes what is essential for his living. This life aids a monk to repent because he is striving to come closer to God as the Only One who can fill and satisfy everyone.

A lay person is troubled by and confesses negative aspects of his life, while a monk targets any deficiency in the positive side of his life and the virtues. He considers it a sin if he were reluctant in praying one of the hourly prayers in the Agpia, or in doing some of his metanias.

THE WILDERNESS IS THE BEST PLACE FOR REPENTANCE

Definitely the wilderness is the most appropriate place for continuous repentance. Let's take some examples:

St Paul The Great Apostle, after the Lord talked to him near Damascus, he believed and was baptised by Ananias and said; "But when it pleased God, who separated me from my mother's womb and called me through His grace to reveal His Son in me, that I might preach Him among the Gentiles, I did not immediately confer with flesh and blood nor did I go up to Jerusalem to those who were apostles before me, but I went to Arabia, and returned again to Damascus." (Galatians 1:15-17). By Arabia he meant the great Arabian desert between Syria and Iraq, where he spent some time offering true repentance for he once was a great Jewish fanatic persecuting the Christians; "and they cast him out of the city and stoned him. And the witnesses laid down their clothes at the feet of a young man called Saul" (Acts 7:58); "Then all who heard were amazed, and said, "Is this not he who destroyed those who called on this name in Jerusalem, and has come here for that purpose, so that he might bring them bound to the chief priests?"(Acts 9:21); "For you have heard of my former conduct in Judaism, how I persecuted the church of God beyond measure and tried to destroy it." (Galatians 1:13).

He spent some time in the desert because he knew it was a place where he can sit with himself, give a sincere account of his deeds, ask for God's mercy and forgiveness and be spiritually charged, ready for the great service he was to begin in preaching the name of the Lord Jesus Christ among the Gentiles.

St Moses The Black, when the Divine Providence prepared him to go to the Scetis desert when he yearned to know the true God. There he became a disciple to St Isidore the priest, where he offered true repentance living a ascetic life with struggles, until he became one of the pillars of the desert and a spiritual father and guide to thousands.

St Mary the Egyptian, after living a sinful life for 17 years, dragging many youth into sin and tempting them, she went to Jerusalem to carry on her sinful acts, yet, when she couldn't enter the church because of an unseen power preventing her, she wept bitterly before St Mary's icon and promised God to live a Godly life if He allowed her to enter the church and have the blessings of the Holy Cross. She then entered the church, offered repentance, confessed her sins to the priest and had Holy Communion. When she was 29, she headed towards the Jordan wilderness, where she spent 47 years in fasting and prayers and become one of the saintly hermits.

Many other saints found the wilderness the most appropriate place to cleanse their souls and purify their life after it was stained with sin.

What are the reasons that make the Desert the Best Place for Repentance?

1. In the monastery, the atmosphere is appropriate for a novice monk to live the life of humility and repentance. He wears a simple robe, living in a humble cell with very little furniture, sometimes doing odd jobs, obeys others and is a student; "But I, like a deaf man, do not hear; and I am like a mute who does not open his mouth. Thus I am like a man who does not hear, and in whose mouth is no response." (Psalm 38:13,14).

2. He is under the guidance of an experienced elder monk, where he sits with him for spiritual advice and guidance, telling him everything in honesty, as a sick person with his doctor, accepting whatever he suggests for his benefit.

15. Monasticism is a Life of Repentance

3. He passes through different tests by the abbot, the elder monks and his confession father, concerning his obedience, humility and tolerance. The atmosphere of being tested is helpful for the repentance of the novice.
4. In the monastery he is not teaching anyone, he is the disciple learning from everyone.

CONTEMPLATION ON THE RITES OF ORDAINING A MONK

The rites of ordaining a monk generally concentrates on:

1. Death to the world
2. The life of repentance
3. Bearing fruits adequate for repentance
4. Carrying the Cross and following the Lord

The first thing in this rite is giving the monk a new name, a name of one of the saints, in order to forget all about his previous life; "that you put off, concerning your former conduct, the old man which grows corrupt according to the deceitful lusts and be renewed in the spirit of your mind".(Ephesians 4:22-24). Also, to take this saint as his intercessor. The new name is given on the eve of ordination, then he spends all night meditating in this new life he is about to start. Next day, after raising the morning incense, he lies on the floor as a dead person before the relics of saints, then they cover all his body, after which the rites of ordination starts. The prayer tunes and the readings are very similar to those of a funeral service, to help fix in the mind of the novice that he has died from the world and its lustful desires; "But those who desire to be rich fall into temptation and a snare, and into many foolish and harmful lusts which drown men in destruction and perdition". (1 Timothy 6:9). The reason for doing this before the relics of the saints is so that their spirit may come upon the monk, as Elisha told his teacher Elijah when he was taken to heaven in a chariot of fire; "And so it was, when they had crossed over, that Elijah said to Elisha, 'Ask! What may I do for you, before I am taken away from you?' and Elisha said, 'Please let a double portion of your spirit be upon me.' So he said, 'You have asked a hard thing. Nevertheless, if you see me when I am taken from you, it shall be so for you; but if not, it shall not be so.' Then it happened as they continued on and talked, that suddenly a chariot of fire appeared with horses of fire, and separated the two of them; and Elijah went up by a whirlwind into heaven." (2 Kings 2: 9-11).

Definitely he will think about death at that moment and this is a great blessing for the monk, encouraging him to think of repentance and to weep bitterly for his sins, having a new vow with God and a new start.

Some of the Readings:

1. Prophecies, encouraging abandoning the world, seeking the eternal life, clinging to the Lord and depending on him.

2. The Trisagion, with its sad tune, glorifying the Ever Living Lord, asking mercy from the Saviour.

3. The Psalm, encouraging repentance and abandoning iniquities; "In you, O Lord, I put my trust; let me never be ashamed; Deliver me in Your righteousness. Bow down Your ear to me, deliver me speedily; be my rock of "refuge", a fortress of defence to save me."

4. The Gospel, calling for self denial for the sake of God, carrying the Cross and following Him to Golgotha; "He said to them: 'whoever desires to come after Me, let him deny himself, and take up his cross, and follow Me.'" (Mark 8:34).

5. The Exposition, the Abbot asks the Lord for the monk saying; "O Lord accept his fasting, prayer, repentance, confession, forgive his sins."

6. In another prayer the Abbot asks the Lord for the sake of the brother saying; "Straighten his ways O Lord, grant him full obedience in order to give up all the natural desires... He who accepted his hair to be cut, help him to cut off all the evil deeds and accept the help of the grace of the Holy Spirit."

7. The brother stands up before the Abbot bowing his head, then the Abbot cuts his hair in 5 places in the shape of a cross, while praying the usual crossings prayer. Cutting the hair is a sign of cutting off the bad thoughts and the devilish tricks.

8. The Abbot then prays on his clothes (the black robe, the qalansewa and the leather girdle) and signs them 3 times as usual.

9. He clothes him with the robe while saying; "Put on the garments of righteousness and the shield of light and bear fruits worthy of

repentance through Jesus Christ our Lord to whom is due glory, forever; Amen."

10. He clothes him with the qalansewa while saying; "Put on the qalansewa of humility and the helmet of salvation".

11. He clothes him with the leather girdle while saying; "Gird yourself with all the bindings of God and the power of repentance, through Jesus Christ our Lord."

12. Then, he reads the commandments for monks, urging him to start his holy struggle and pure monastic life; "Keep the covenant which you vowed now, worship God in awe and reverence, pray the Psalms and watch during the night, pray the Psalmody (i.e. be regular in the daily midnight praise) and all the church's prayers. Do this eagerly, with moderate fasting, asceticism and purity of the body, in order to be a friend to the pure angels. Be obedient and submissive, listen to him who guides you towards the path of God and His Commandments to the extent of death, so that you might gain the crown of the children of God, and inherit the heavenly kingdom, and have a share and inheritance with all the saints who pleased God ever since the beginning"

13. The new monk attends the Holy Liturgy and partakes of the Holy Sacraments.

It is a wonderful rite, even meditating in its procedures gives awe and makes one zealous for the life of virtue and repentance. The monk now starts a new life; "Therefore, if anyone is in Christ, he is a new creation; old things have passed away, behold, all things have become new." (2 Corinthians 5:17).

16. Monasticism is a Life of Pilgrimage and Death to the World

Monasticism is a life of pilgrimage, of being a stranger in the world with all its belongings and a readiness to dwell in the heavenly dwelling with all its blessings and grace. The prophecies read in the rite of ordaining a monk reminds the monk of Abraham the father of fathers who spent all his life as a pilgrim, living in tents, waiting to dwell in the city, whose founder and establisher is God. God told Abraham; "Get out of your country, from your kindred, and from your father's house to a land that I will show you. I will make you a great nation; I will bless you and make your name great; and you shall be a blessing. I will bless those who bless you, and I will curse him who curses you; and in you all the families of the earth shall be blessed." (Genesis 12:1-3).

So Abraham obeyed the Divine Voice; "By faith Abraham obeyed when he was called to go out to the place which he would afterward receive as an inheritance. And he went out, not knowing where he was going." (Hebrews 11:8). Abraham and all the great fathers, the heroes of faith, were pilgrims; "These all died in faith, not having received the promises, but having seen them afar off were assured of them, embraced them, and confessed that they were strangers and pilgrims on the earth. For those who say such things declare plainly that they seek a homeland. And truly if they had called to mind that country from which they had come out, they would have had opportunity to return. But now they desire a better, that is, a heavenly country. Therefore God is not ashamed to be called their God, for He has prepared a city for them." (Hebrews 11:13-16).

When Pharaoh asked Jacob his age, he answered; "the days of the years of my pilgrimage are one hundred and thirty years; few and evil have been the days of the years of my life, and they have not attained to the days of the years of the life of my fathers in the days of their pilgrimage." (Genesis 47:9). Job the Righteous says; "Now my days are swifter than a runner; they flee away, they see no good." (Job 9:25). David felt the estrangement and the vanity of the world; "For we are aliens and pilgrims before You, as were all our fathers; Our days on earth are as a shadow and without hope: (1 Chronicles 29:15). Also; "My days are like a shadow that lengthens, and I wither away like grass." (Psalm 102:11). Thus the abbot asks the Lord to teach the monk His Commandments in order to learn and practice them and be ready for the everlasting life; "I am a stranger in the earth; do not hide Your commandments from me" (Psalm 119:19). St Paul in his eagerness for eternal life says; "We are confident, yes, well pleased rather to be absent from the body and to be present with the Lord." (2 Corinthians 5:8).

The Concept of Pilgrimage According to a Layman and a Monk

For a layman pilgrimage means not to love money and wealth, not to love his wife or children more than God even though he lives with them. St Paul advises the laymen to control themselves during their life of pilgrimage and to prepare for the eternal residence; "But this I say, brethren, the time is short, so that from now on even those who have wives should be as though they had none, those who weep as though they did not weep, those who rejoice as though they did not rejoice, those who buy as though they did not possess, and those who use this world as not misusing it. For the form of this world is passing away. But I want you to be without care. He who is unmarried cares for the things that belong to the Lord – how he may please the Lord" (1 Corinthians 7:29-32). Also St Peter says; "Beloved, I beg you as sojourners and pilgrims, abstain from fleshly lusts which war against the soul." (1 Peter 2:11); "And if you call on the Father, who without partiality judges according to each one's work, conduct yourselves throughout the time of your sojourning here in fear." (1 Peter 1:17).

16. Monasticism is a Life of Pilgrimage and Death to the World

As for the monk, pilgrimage is at a higher level than that which pertains to any other believer. It is true death to the world. The rite of ordaining monks contains prayers for the departed, to remind the monk that he is actually dead to the world and to remember that he can die at any time and thus should be ready for that moment. Monasticism is based on a chosen death to the world, before the compulsory death of the body.

We read in the life of St Anthony, the father of monks, when his father departed, he looked at his fathers' body and said; "Blessed be the name of the Lord. Isn't this body intact, all that has changed is the breathing has stopped. So where is your might and great power? Where is all the money that you kept collecting? You have left everything. Now, you left without your choice, but I'll leave by my own choice." Then he headed to the desert saying, "I'll not do like my father, I choose to leave this world willingly."

The same happened with St Paul the first hermit, after the departure of his father, he disagreed with his brother concerning the inheritance and how to divide it between them. On their way to the Governor to decide for them, they saw the funeral of a rich man. One of the attendants told St Paul that this person was so rich, but now he would just be buried, leaving all his wealth behind. St Paul then returned and didn't go to the Governor but instead he headed to the Eastern desert according to the angel's guidance where he lived for 90 years. God provided for him through a crow that brought him half a loaf of bread daily.

A great example of dying to the world is St Arsenius, who always remembered death and was crying at all times. Even at the time of his departure, he said; "the fear of this moment never departed me since I became a monk."

According to a monk 'death to the world' means to shut his inner and outer sense to anything happening in the world. A dead man leaves his parents, friends and beloved ones and it is the same with a monk. He leaves everything behind and clings to the Lord, repeating with the Apostle; "Therefore, from now on, we regard no one according to the flesh. Even though we have known Christ according to the flesh, yet now we know Him thus no longer." (2 Corinthians 5:16), also; "And a man's foes will be those of his own household" (Matthew 10:36).

A dead man doesn't eat, drink or enjoy anything in life and a monk eats just what's enough to keep him living and wears a simple black robe. We can't hear the voice of a dead man and he has no more power or might over others. A monk should be exactly the same.

Everything in the monastery reminds a monk of death. He also remembers death in his cell, thus he will think twice before committing a sin. The tomb of the Lord Jesus was described as follows; "Then he took it down, wrapped it in linen, and laid it in a tomb that was hewn out of the rock, where no one had ever lain before." (Luke 23:53); also the tomb of Lazarus; "Then Jesus, again groaning in Himself, came to the tomb. It was a cave, and a stone lay against it." (John 11:38). It is true that, 'the monks like to be buried alive on earth, rather than to be dead and buried in Hades.'

A dead man is silent and a monk should be characterised by his silence. St John the Short says; "Silence in everything is true pilgrimage." St John Saba, the Spiritual elder says; "He who controls his mouth, can also control the temptations. The mouth of a silent person can interpret the Mysteries of God."

A dead person is not proud of his wealth, his parents or his former glory, he never cares about honour or disgrace. A monk must be the same, he should tolerate everything thankfully.

The Fathers' Sayings about Pilgrimage and Death to the World

St Macarius the Great considers pilgrimage the primary means by which the saints reach high spiritual levels. He says; "Great is the glory of the saints. They did not buy it with the riches of the world, or with being excellent in a trade or position, but they were estranged to this world, lived in poverty and hunger. Thus I see that they gained this great glory because they submitted themselves totally to God. They abandoned all desires for the sake of the Love of the Lord, they carried the cross and followed Him. Nothing had separated them from God's love."

"Those who decide to become monks have to deny everything in this world and ignore any beauty in the world, so that they establish a perfect foundation for their monasticism." St John Climacus

"It is not good to feel sorry for anything that you abandoned in the world. This can attract us gradually to the world and quench our pilgrimage. It is impossible for a person to look with one eye to heaven and with the other to the ground. It is also impossible to be a stranger to the world while your heart and mind are in the world." St John Climacus

"Those who abandoned the world and its desires became pilgrims, tolerating the temptations and enjoying grief, hating the desires and luxury of the world. They left their houses in order to dwell in the house of the Lord forever. They left parents, brothers, sisters in order that the Lord might be their Father, Mother, Sister and Brother." St John Saba

"Blessed are You O Beloved Lord because You are Everything for us, with You, we need nothing else." St John Saba

"Blessed is he who never talks about worldly things in order to talk with You, because You reveal Yourself to him and comfort him. You are with him at all times. He enjoys Your Light; You become his food, drink, and cover. You make his heart rejoice. He closes his door for You to open Your door for him. He leaves everyone and sits with You. You enlighten his mind so he can comprehend Your Mysteries. The desire of the world within him is changed into the desire to live with You. The aroma of grace from Your Holy Body replaces all the other perfumes of the world. When he eats, he sees You in the bread, when he drinks, he feels that You are the Rock of which Living Water springs." St John Saba

THE REAL FAMILY OF A MONK

"Let your father be the person who can toil with you and tolerate your sins. Your mother should be the awesome one who is capable of washing and cleaning you. Your brother should be the one who supports you and helps you to reach high spiritual levels. Your wife (which you can never abandon) should be the continuous remembrance of death. Your beloved children should be your heart sighs. Let your body be your slave. Make friends with the hosts who could be of benefit to you at the moment of your departure (the angels and saints)." St John Climacus

17. Monasticism is a Life of Consecration

There are two main calls for consecration in our beloved church:

1. Priesthood
2. Monasticism

A priest is called to work for the salvation of souls by performing the Holy Sacraments for the believers, preaching, guiding, visitation, solving problems, etc., as a king, father and delegate of God. Lord Jesus has given him His own congregation to lead them; "For you were like sheep going astray, but have now returned the Shepherd and Overseer of your souls." (1 Peter 2:25).

So the priest consecrates his life totally to serve the congregation as Lord Jesus says; "And for their sakes I sanctify Myself, that they also may be sanctified by the truth." (John 17:19). As for the monk, he consecrates himself to reach a high spiritual level, become united with God, purify his heart and consequently gain the salvation of his soul. His lifestyle is to live in the wilderness and desert, pray, meditate and gradually reach a higher level of ecstasy and unity with God beyond any measure.

A monk gradually increases in the life of repentance, purity of heart, serenity of mind and senses, he reaches a state of clairvoyance and peace which makes him live in heaven, while he is still on earth. This is known as 'the token of heaven' granted to the strong strugglers.

A monk who keeps struggling in his cell, in fasting, prayers, praises, following the commandments and conquering the worldly desires could, through the grace of God, gain eternal life with those who pleased the Lord ever since the beginning.

A monk in this case resembles a whole burnt offering; "And the priest shall burn all on the altar as a burnt sacrifice, an offering made by fire, a sweet aroma to the Lord." (Leviticus 1:9). He is a person whose heart is blazing with the love of Lord Jesus, saying with the Psalmist; "As the deer pants for the water brooks, So pants my soul for You, O God. My soul thirsts for God, the living God, when shall I come and appear before God?" (Psalm 42:1-2).

18. Monasticism is a Life of Prayer

One of the blessings God granted the church is a special order of Christians devoted to prayer and worship; that's the monastic life. As St John Climacus says; "Prayer is the wealth of monks, the food of those living in a spiritual life, the weapon of the silent ones."

Prayer is the main aspect of the monks life. Monks start gradually with prayers, then meditation, ecstasy, contemplation until they reach a very high level of partnership with the Lord. Prayer in the life of a monk differentiates them from laymen. Lay people may be too busy with work and family commitments to be able to live a life of prayer. In order to be free to pray without distraction, the early monks chose to live in the deserts and wilderness, in spite of the harsh conditions of these places. They chose to live a life of continuous contemplation on God, away from any distractions that would separate them from God, "earnestly serving God night and day" (Acts 26:7); a perfect choice because the calmness and serenity of the wilderness helps them to reach the highest level of enjoying life with the Lord.

Lord Jesus Christ is the Founder of Life in the Wilderness

Our Lord Jesus Christ used to spend much time in the wilderness, in solitude and prayer. It is written in the Bible that He went to the mountains when He fasted for 40 days and nights and conquered Satan exposing his tricks. Even during His service, He frequently went alone to the mountains at night; "And in the daytime He was teaching in the temple, but at night He went out and stayed on the mountain called Olivet." (Luke 21:37), and; "Now it came to pass in those days that He went out to the mountain to pray, and continued all night in prayer to God." (Luke 6:12).

ABRAHAM LOVED DWELLING IN THE MOUNTAINS

Abraham, the father of fathers, when he came to the land of Canaan, yearned to live in the mountains, with its spiritual release and purity of prayers so; "he moved from there to the mountain east of Bethel, and he pitched his tent with Bethel on the west and Ai on the east; there he built an altar to the Lord and called on the name of the Lord." (Genesis 12:8). Also, when he came back from Egypt; "Then Abram went up from Egypt, he and his wife and all that he had, and Lot with him, to the South. Abram was very rich in livestock, in sliver, and in gold. And he went on his journey from the South as far as Bethel, to the place where his tent had been at the beginning between Bethel and Ai, to the place of the altar that he had made there at first. And there Abram called on the name of the Lord." (Genesis 13:1-4).

GOD ASKED HIS PEOPLE TO WORSHIP HIM IN THE WILDERNESS

When the Lord sent Moses and Aaron to Pharaoh to release the children of Israel, they said to Pharaoh; " Thus says the Lord God of Israel: Let My people go, that they may hold a feast to Me in the wilderness" (Exodus 5:1). When Pharaoh refused, the Lord sent them again to him; "Go to Pharaoh in the morning, when he goes out to the water, and you shall stand by the river's bank to meet him; and the rod which was turned to a serpent you shall take in your hand. And you shall say to him, 'The Lord God of the Hebrews has sent me to you, saying, 'Let My people go, that they may serve Me in the wilderness; but indeed until now you would not hear!'". (Exodus 7:15-16). This was repeated several times in Exodus 8:2, 8:20, 9:1, 9:13. Pharaoh said to Moses; "Go, sacrifice to your God in the land" (Exodus 8:25); they refused and answered; "It is not right to do so, for we would be sacrificing the abomination of the Egyptians to the Lord our God. If we sacrifice the abomination of the Egyptians before their eyes, then will they not stone us? We will go three days' journey into the wilderness and sacrifice to the Lord our God, as He will command us. And Pharaoh said, 'I will let you go, that you may sacrifice to the

18. Monasticism is a Life of Prayer

Lord your God in the wilderness; only you shall not go very far away. Intercede for me'". (Exodus 8:26-28). Hence God has pleasure in worship offered to Him in the wilderness because God is; "Rejoicing in His inhabited world, and my delight was with the sons of men" (Proverbs 8:31), out of His great love to mankind. Consequently, He wants the human beings to enjoy His company and feel His goodness, love and blessings by being in His presence through pure prayers raised to him. The wilderness with its calm quiet atmosphere is the best place from which a person can offer God such pure prayers.

SOME MONKS REACHED HIGH SPIRITUAL LEVELS OF PRAYERS

Monks are famous for their patience, struggle and ascetism. Some monks have reached a level where Jesus is their closest friend and brother, as did Moses the prophet; "I speak with him face to face, even plainly, and not in dark sayings; and he sees the form of the Lord. Why then were you not afraid to speak against My servant Moses." (Numbers 12:8). Some reached the level of Abraham to who God revealed His secrets; "And the Lord said, "Shall I hide from Abraham what I am doing" (Genesis 18:17). God also accepted Abraham's intercession for Sodom and Gomorrah, though He did not find even ten righteous people as Abraham had asked. St Macarius of Alexandria kept praying for three whole days, and finally the devil out of jealousy burnt the rug on which he was standing.

We also read about St Maximos and St Domadios that their prayers were ascending out of their mouths like strings of fire. St Arsenius used to pray all night, beginning at sunset of Saturday he would pray with his arms stretched out until sunrise on Sunday.

THE POWER OF THE SAINTS' PRAYERS

- The prayers of St Tadros of Scetis used to bind the devils outside his cell.
- The prayers of St Macarius the Great and St Sarabamoun revived dead men.
- The prayers of St Macarius of Alexandria caused strong rain to fall after a long period of drought.
- Many miracles took place as a result of the prayers of saints and Cross-bearers.

A very touching story about the power of prayers is written in the Sinaxarium of 25th Abib about the life of the martyr St Apakragon; "he was a robber, and one day, together with two other robbers they decided to go and steal from the cell of a monk in El Scetis desert. When they went at night, they found him praying, so they decided to wait outside his cell till he finishes and sleeps. Yet after a while they became very tired. In the morning, the elder monk came out, so they left their weapons and bowed at his feet. The elder preached them and they became monks. The elder then announced to St Apakragon, who toiled in many struggles and asceticism, that he will become a martyr. He gained the crown of martyrdom after being a robber."

Their Mouths Were Sanctified Because They Continuously Talk with God

They prayed without ceasing, even while doing their handwork. They were always reading the Holy Bible and spiritual books, using what they learn as a material for their prayers. Although they were poor, yet everyone honoured them, they lived an angelic life.

The Great Fathers of the Church Witness That the Monks were Men of Prayer

When Pope Benjamin the first was consecrating the altar of the church of St Macarius, he said: "while I was giving the Holy Communion to the monks I saw a great vision which I should not conceal. I saw incense coming out of their mouths when partaking of the Holy Communion. Then the ceiling of the church was split, and the incense ascended. I noticed the incense coming out of their mouths with their prayers while approaching the Communion, thus I was sure that their prayers were accepted by God. I also saw the angels carrying their prayers and presenting them before the Throne of the Father. I praised the Lord and thanked him for making me worthy to see what I had seen."

Pope Athanasius the Apostolic also praised the monks saying: "The cells of monks were considered altars of praise, where you hear Psalms and spiritual hymns. Righteousness and love were prevailing, with continuous prayer and fasting. The monks used to satisfy their needs through their handwork, so that they might not become a burden on anyone else. They despised the riches of this world and those who visited the monasteries came back amazed as if they had seen angels, not human beings."

St Ironimus also praised monks saying: "they never care about shelter, food or clothes. They just look for the coming of Lord Jesus, their Refuge. If anyone was in need of something that he didn't have, he just lifted up his arms to his heavenly Father and by the end of his prayers, he found all his needs available to him."

All the inhabitants of Egypt knew that God was preserving the monks and that there was plenty of goodness because of the monks prayers.

As a result of their prayers and the Divine angelic life these monks were living, many emperors and kings sought their blessings and guidance. We read about the Great Emperor Constantine, that he sent a gentle letter to St Anthony asking the saints' blessings and prayers for himself and his family. St Theodosius the Great consulted St John of Assuit in great matters concerning the country. The Roman leader who was encamping in Aswan also used to ask St John's guidance. This saint was called "the Prophet of Egypt" at that time. Emperor Theodosius Junior also sent two letters to the elders of Scetis, asking them to pray to God for granting him a child to be his successor on the throne.

THIS IS NOT SOMETHING NEW, BECAUSE WE HAVE SIMILAR EXAMPLES IN THE OLD TESTAMENT

1. **Pharaoh asking Moses and Aaron:** He asked Moses and Aaron many times; "Then Pharaoh called for Moses and Aaron, and said: 'Entreat the Lord that he may take away the frogs from me and from my people; and I will let the people go, that they may sacrifice to the Lord.'" (Exodus 8:8); "Entreat the Lord, that there may be no more mighty thundering and hail, for it is enough, I will let you go, and you shall stay no longer."(Exodus 9:28); and "Now therefore, please forgive my sin only this once, and entreat the Lord your God that He may take away from me this death only." (Exodus 10:17).

2. **The people asking Samuel the Prophet:** When the children of Israel asked for a king, Samuel informed them that the Lord's wrath has fallen on them: "So Samuel called to the Lord, and the Lord sent thunder and rain that day; and all the people greatly feared the Lord and Samuel. And all the people said to Samuel, "Pray for your servants to the Lord Your God, that we may not die; for we have added to all our sins the evil of asking a king for ourselves." (1 Samuel 12:18-19).

3. Hezekiah the king asking Isaiah the Prophet: When king Hezekiah knew about Rabshakeh the commander of the Assyrian army, who was threatening them; "And so it was, when King Hezekiah heard it, that he tore his clothes, covered himself with sackcloth, and went into the house of the Lord. Then he sent Eliakim, who was over the household, Shebna the scribe, and the elders of the priests, covered with sackcloth, to Isaiah the prophet, the son of Amoz. And they said to him: "Thus says Hezekiah; 'This day is a day of trouble, and rebuke, and blasphemy; for the children have come to birth, but there is no strength to bring them forth. It may be that the Lord your God will hear all the words of the Rabshakeh, whom his master the king of Assyria has sent to reproach the living God, and will reprove the words which the Lord your God has heard. Therefore lift up your prayer for the remnant that is left'" (2 Kings 19:1-4).

4. Josiah the King asks the Priests: When Josiah heard the script of Moses' Law and found that the people had deviated totally from following it, "Then the king commanded Hilkiah the priest, Ahikam the son of Shaphan, Achbor the son of Michaiah, Shaphn the scribe, and Asaiah a servant of the king, saying, "Go, inquire of the Lord for me, for the people and for all Judah, concerning the words of this book that has been found; for great is the wrath of the Lord that is aroused against us, because our fathers have not obeyed the words of this book, to do according to all that is written concerning us." (2 Kings 22:12-13).

5. Zedekiah the king asks Jeremiah the Prophet: After becoming the king of Jerusalem; "Zedekiah the king sent Jehucal the son of Shelemiah, and Zephaniah the son of Maaseiah, the priest, to the prophet Jeremiah, saying, Pray now to the Lord our God for us." (Jeremiah 37:3).

And so, in all ages and everywhere people resort to the men of prayers who have a strong companionship with God, asking them to pray to God on their behalf. Many times God is glorified, accepting their prayers and healing a disease or solving a problem.

THE POWER OF THE PRAYERS OF THE MONKS

The monks didn't reach this level of spirituality because they have a different nature than ours, or more gifts or talents, but simply because they perfected the conditions of the acceptable prayer. Examples of these conditions are:

1. Faith: Which assures that God listens to every word that they say; He responds according to His good will.

Father Nestarion says; "Make sure that you stand daily before God without sin. Pray to God as if you can see Him physically, because he is truly present."

Another elder says; "Because my brethren, you should stand before God blameless. Approach Him with tears like the sinful woman. Plead to Him as if he is standing before you because He is so close to us and so caring." They believed in God "For from the top of the rocks I see him, and from the hills I behold him; there! A people dwelling alone, not reckoning itself among the nations." (Numbers 23:9). They had the simple strong faith that can move the mountain, "So Jesus said to them, 'Because of your unbelief; for assuredly, I say to you, if you have faith as a mustard seed, you will say to this mountain, 'Move from here to there', and it will move; and nothing will be impossible for you.'" (Matthew 17:20); "So the Lord said, 'If you have faith as a mustard seed, you can say to this mulberry tree, 'Be pulled up by the roots and be planted in the sea, and it would obey you.'" (Luke 17:6).

The Paradise of The Holy Fathers tell this story about St Moses the Black, "One day, some monks went to visit him in his cell in the mountain. He cooked some lentils for them, but he didn't have enough water. He kept going in and out several times praying to God until it started raining, and his pot was full of water. When the monks asked him about the reason for going in and out, he answered: "I was praying to the Lord saying: Lord You brought me to this place and I have no water to cook for your servants"".

Anba Dolas retells this story about his teacher Anba Bessarion, "Once, we were walking by a lake and I was thirsty, so he prayed and asked me to drink. When I drank from the lake, it was normal drinking water, so I started filling the bottles thinking I might feel thirst again. But St Bessarion said to me: 'May the Lord forgive you my son for doing this because He is the One who guides us, He looks after us everywhere.'"

2. Love: They were filled with love towards each other; "Since you have purified your souls in obeying the truth through the spirit in sincere love of the brethren, love one another fervently with a pure heart." (1 Peter 1:22). They never keep any hatred or envy in their hearts, they forgive each other, are merciful and do metanias in humility to the extent that they burn the devils; "Be angry and do not sin; do not let the sun go down on your wrath" (Ephesians 4:26) and; "Therefore I desire that the men pray everywhere, lifting up holy hands, without wrath and doubting" (1 Timothy 2:8).

3. Obeying and Following the Commandments: They used to study the Holy Bible and follow its Commandments. They turned these commandments into life; each one of them was a fifth Gospel. They proved their great love to Lord Jesus; "He who has My commandments and keeps them, it is he who loves me. And he who loves Me will be loved by My Father, and I will love him and manifest Myself to him." (John 14:21), thus the Lord truly loved them and accepted their prayers as the Apostle says; "And whatever we ask we received from Him, because we keep His commandments and do those things that are pleasing in His sight." (1 John 3:22).

4. Mercy: "Whoever shuts his ears to the cry of the poor will also cry himself and not be heard" (Proverbs 21:13). Also there is no mercy on Judgement Day to those who did not have mercy on others. The father saints reached a level of having mercy on others, to the point of selling themselves as slaves to give money to the poor, like St Bebnouda and St Peter the Worshipper. Another one gave the only loaf of bread to a poor person, and he was without food for three days, giving thanks to God.

5. Fasting: If we resemble prayer to a flying eagle, so his wings are fasting and alms giving, with which it is lifted up to heaven. Fasting calms down the body and the senses. It puts a limit to vain talk, thus a person becomes ready for spiritual prayer. The soul then is released from the slavery of the body and keeps meditating on Eternal life.

Some fathers used to fast for a week, or 3 days in a row. Some of them fasted completely from certain types of food, which they considered a kind of luxury for their bodies. They used to eat humble meals, just to keep their bodies operating. They perfected countless conditions for the acceptable prayer, till their prayers became so powerful, never returning empty.

H.H. Pope Shenouda III praises the angelic monastic life by saying; "The life of the monks is a blessing to the whole world. They offer their lives as a burning sacrifice in joy and love. God's wrath is withdrawn because of them because amidst the world, which is full of sin and wickedness, God sees a sample of human saints, consecrated just for Him; they left everything because of His Love. A prayer of one monk protects thousands even ten thousands of human beings if it is coming out of a pure heart, truly clinging to the Lord."

The Three Saints Abba Macarius

19. Monasticism is a Life of Discipleship

The Discipleship of the Apostles

Christianity is based on discipleship. Lord Jesus chose His disciples who lived with Him and followed Him everywhere, watching closely His life of virtue and perfection. They saw Him in fervent deep prayers, so their hearts became inflamed for prayer; "And it came to pass, as He was praying in a certain place, when He ceased, that one of His disciples said to Him, 'Lord, teach us to pray, as John also taught his disciples.'" (Luke 11:1), so He taught them that powerful prayer, which is charged with Divine power, full of spirituality; "So He said to them, 'when you pray, say: Our Father in heaven, hallowed by Your name. Your kingdom come, Your will be done on earth as it is in heaven. Give us day by day our daily bread. And forgive us our sins, for we also forgive everyone who is indebted to us. And do not lead us into temptation, but deliver us from the evil one.'" (Luke 11:2-4). It is also written; "And it happened, as He was alone praying, that His disciples joined Him, and He asked them, saying, "Who do the crowds say that I am?" (Luke 9:18). Which means that Lord Christ used to talk to His disciples even in His solitude.

They saw Him blessing the food, they learned from Him how to break the bread and the protocol of eating. After the Resurrection, when He met the two disciples on the way to Emmaus; "Now it came to pass, as he sat at the table with them, that He took bread, blessed and broke it, and gave it to them. Then their eyes were opened and they knew Him, and he vanished from their sight." (Luke 24:30-31). They discovered the Lord by the way He broke the bread, which is the same way that He taught the disciples to break bread.

They saw Him healing the sick, comforting the grieved, having mercy on the sinners and the tax collectors, visiting their houses and eating with them, attracting them to believe in Him for the salvation of their souls and disregarding the mockings and accusations of the Jews for mingling with those people. They saw Him sharing with the joyous, blessing the wedding at Cana of Galilee, sharing with the grieved, crying with Mary and Martha for the death of Lazarus their brother, comforting the widow of Nain by reviving her only son and many others whom the Holy Bible did not mention. They saw His tolerance and longsuffering with the Pharisees and Scribes and listened to His wise answers to their deceitful questions.

So they learned all these virtues from Him, not only through His words and teachings but also through His good example and perfect divine personality.

He disclosed to His disciples the secrets of His coming to the world, calling them His beloved; "No longer do I call you servants, for a servant does not know what his master is doing; but I have called you friends, for all things that I heard from My Father I have made known to you." (John 15:15), also; "And He said, 'to you it has been given to know the mysteries of the kingdom of God, but to the rest it is given in parables'". (Luke 8:10); "But without a parable he did not speak to them. And when they were alone, He explained all things to His disciples." (Mark 4:34). Thus His faithful disciples kept clinging to Him during the period of His service on earth, learning from His words and deeds, His struggles and His virtues. They became true disciples to Lord Jesus who established the foundations of honest discipleship as a basis for the Christian life.

After the Resurrection, the Great Teacher gathered His beloved disciples once again, he completed the period of discipleship and teaching; "to whom He also presented Himself alive after His suffering by many infallible proofs, being seen by them during forty days and speaking of the things pertaining to the kingdom of God. And being assembled together with them, He commanded them not to depart from Jerusalem, but to wait for the Promise of the Father, which He said, you have heard from Me." (Acts 1:3,4). After the descent of the Holy Spirit and gaining the required power for preaching and teaching, they started their preaching; "Go therefore and make disciples of all the nations, baptizing them in the name of the Father and of the Son and of the Holy Spirit, teaching them to observe all things that I have commanded you; and lo, I am with you always, even to the end of the age. Amen." (Matt 28:19,20). Thus, He ordered them to make other disciples, as they had been His disciples.

Paul and Barnabas were also Disciples, the most distinguished disciples after the twelve Apostles. When the Lord talked to Saul of Tarsus (Paul) near Damascus and blamed him for persecuting the Christians, Saul asked the Lord what to do. Instead of the Lord instructing St Paul, He guided him to a spiritual father who would teach him and make him a disciple; that was Ananias who himself was a disciple.

On the other hand, the Lord said to Ananias in a vision; "Arise and go to the street called Straight, and inquire at the house of Judas for one called Saul of Tarsus, for behold, he is praying." (Acts 9:11), "And Ananias went his way and entered the house; and laying his hands on him he said, 'Brother Saul, the Lord Jesus, who appeared to you on the road as you came, has sent me that you may receive your sight and be filled with the Holy Spirit.' Immediately there fell from his eyes something like scales, and he received his sight at once; and he arose and was baptized." (Acts 9:17-18). After this successful discipleship, St Paul; "Immediately he preached the Christ in the synagogues, that he is the Son of God. Then all who heard were amazed, and said, 'is this not he who destroyed those who called on this name in Jerusalem, and has come here for that purpose, so that he might bring them bound to the chief priests?'" (Acts 9:20-21). Then Paul and Barnabas; "And when they had preached the gospel to that city and made many disciples, they returned to Lystra, Iconium and Antioch." (Acts 14:21). Thus, he who is a disciple of the elders, learning the basics of spiritual life and faith, is the only one who can later be a spiritual father and trustee of other souls guiding and teaching them.

OBSTACLES OF TRUE DISCIPLESHIP IN THE WORLD

The number of believers is so huge, while the pastors are few; "Then He said to His disciples, 'the harvest truly is plentiful, but the labourers are few.'" (Matthew 9:37). Also there are so many responsibilities and duties for pastors, thus discipleship has weakened. A pastor cannot easily know everyone by name, giving him/her the suitable spiritual nourishment at the time it is needed. Amongst all these obstacles in carrying out discipleship properly, monasticism has preserved the original rites of discipleship, thus it is a source of blessing and salvation of many souls.

Discipleship is the Secret of Strength in Monasticism

"The secret of the strength and flourishing of monasticism in the early centuries was the system of discipleship followed. The sweet aroma of our Lord Christ, which was in the hearts of the fathers in the wilderness attracted many who became disciples to the Lord. That was why the deserts and wilderness were filled with thousands of saintly monks." One of the fathers

"A novice is given to a spiritual father to become his disciple. He teaches and guides him. His only concern is to lift the novice up to perfection, teaching him how to conquer his desires." St John Cassian

The first lesson to a novice tutored by his spiritual father is to deny his will and submit it totally to his tutor. The Lord often blessed the obedience of the novice monks to their spiritual fathers and this was revealed through miracles. The miracles performed from the obedient novice deepens the spiritual value of being obedient and makes him more eager to practise it. These rules were applied in the wilderness of Scetis, where each group of monks were under the supervision of one of the elders, following St Paul's words; "Obey those who rule over you, and be submissive, for they watch out for your souls, as those who must give account. Let them do so with joy and not with grief, for that would be unprofitable for you." (Hebrews 13:17). A monk once asked an elder father for a word of benefit, so he said to him; "My son, if you want to be a farmer, how could you learn this without living for a while with a farmer, learning all about planting, irrigation, harvesting, etc.. It is exactly the same with monasticism, how can you learn about monasticism if you are not guided by an elder? If you keep moving from one place to another, or just lived alone, you will spend your whole life without gaining any virtues. You should be a disciple to an elder, to get his final blessing, like Elisha who stayed with Elijah till he was lifted up to heaven, when he blessed Elisha, he got double of Elijah's spirit."

*St Bemwa (Pambo) told the elders before his departure about St John the Short who accompanied him; "This is an angel, not a human being." St John who obeyed St Balamoun his father and brought to him the hyena and

many other great works. Now, look what happened to Esau when he left his father and mingled with the nations whom God rejected; Gehazi was hit by leprosy when he didn't obey Elisha; the disciples who left Jesus destroyed their souls.

Here, I have told you about the way of life and death. If you enter through the narrow gate, which is obedience to your father, you will reach eternal life, if you choose the wide gate, which is your own desires, you will surely perish.

Examples of Great Disciples

Discipleship is not restricted to a certain age, we can always learn and be disciples. Joshua the son of Nun was Moses' disciple and servant until Moses' departure and he became the leader after Moses, according to the Lord's order (Joshua 1:1,2). The Lord even encouraged him; "No man shall be able to stand before you all the days of your life; as I was with Moses, so I will be with you. I will not leave you nor forsake you." (Joshua 1:5).

Elisha was Elijah's disciple until the latter was lifted up alive to heaven; "And so it was, when they had crossed over, that Elijah said to Elisha, 'Ask! What may I do for you, before I am taken away from here?' And Elisha said, 'Please let a double portion of your spirit be upon me.' So he said, 'You have asked a hard thing, Nevertheless if you see me when I am taken from you, it shall be so for you; but if not, it shall not be so.'"(2 Kings 2:9-10).

The disciples of St John the Baptist accompanied their teacher all the period of his service, even when he was jailed they were close to him. When Herod cut his head off; "Then his disciples came and took away the body and buried it, and went and told Jesus." (Matthew 14:12).

The Lord Jesus' Apostles accompanied Him till His ascension to heaven; "Now it came to pass, while he blessed them, that he was parted from them and carried up into heaven." (Luke 24:51).

Some Distinguished Disciples in Monasticism

- St Paphnutius, the disciple of St Macarius the Great, became a spiritual leader after him in leading the brethren.

- St John the Short, the honest disciple and servant of St Pambo. Later he became the "Priest of Scetis".

We hear in the Holy Liturgy and in the commemoration of saints; "St

Pachomius the Father of community, and St Theodore his disciple; St Shenouda the Archimandrite and St Wissa his disciple; St Samuel the Confessor and Justus and Apollo his disciples." Usually these great disciples succeeded their teachers in guiding and teaching in the same manner and spirit which they have learnt.

THE BLESSING OF DISCIPLESHIP

St Gregory the Theologian says; "My brother, leave the high positions to those who love them and come down. Be like me, I preferred to be a lad and a disciple all my life." He said these words because of his strong belief in the blessings of being a disciple to an experienced elder. Some of these blessings are:

1. **Continuous growth:** in learning about fasting, prayer, love and mercy. Following the Bible's words; "Remember the days of old, consider the years of many generations. Ask your father, and he will show you; your elders and they will tell you." (Deuteronomy 32:7).

2. **Humility:** Discipleship keeps the person humble, always feeling that he is young, under the supervision of someone else. Through humility, a person is lifted up to perfection. This story is written in "The Paradise of The Holy Fathers": "A father monk said that he saw 4 ranks in heaven:

   i. An ill person living the life of patience and thanksgiving.

   ii. A person hosting strangers and helping the poor and weak.

   iii. A person living in solitude struggling in the wilderness.

   iv. A disciple obeying his father for the sake of God.

   He saw that the disciple was the highest above all the other three, so he asked the angel, "How come the disciple is the highest although he is the youngest?" So he was answered: "Everyone of the other three is doing good according to his own free will, but this disciple is denying his will and obeying his teacher for the sake of God – this is the best virtue."

3. **One Thought and One Spirit** among the whole group. Thus there are no divisions, no envy but rather unity of the monks living together in love and peace; "God sets the solitary in families; He brings out

those who are bound into prosperity; but the rebellious dwell in a dry land." (Psalm 68:6). The solitary here means those who have one thought and one heart, like the believers of the early church.

4. **An Upright Path:** The life of discipleship guarantees – with the Grace of God – eternal life. It is exactly like a person so confident in the middle of the sea, being carried by someone else. Whenever he is about to fall, he can seek guidance and instruction to direct him to the right path. It is written; " Two are better than one, because they have a good reward for their labour. For if they fall, one will lift up his companion. But woe to him who is alone when he falls, for he has no one to help him up" (Ecclesiastes 4:9-10). Also; "Though one may be overpowered by another, two can withstand him, and a threefold cord is not quickly broken." (Ecclesiastes 4:12); and; "Where there is no counsel, the people fall; but in the multitude of counsellors there is safety." (Proverbs 11:14).

5. **Peace and Safety:** It guarantees a peaceful and safe spiritual life; "My brethren, let not many of you become teachers, knowing that we shall receive a stricter judgment" (James 3:1), also; "Therefore, my beloved brethren, let every man be swift to hear, slow to speak, slow to wrath." (James 1:19), and; "Then Samuel said: 'Has the Lord as great delight in burnt offerings and sacrifices, as in obeying the voice of the Lord: Behold, to obey is better than sacrifice, and to heed than the fat of rams.'" (1 Samuel 15:22).

20. Monasticism is a Life of Fulfilling the Commandments

The true monk is dead to the world, walking in the monastic path, able to fulfill the commandments of God with no obstacles whatsoever. St Augustine says; "I sat on the top of the world when I felt that I do not fear anything or desire anything." If a monk fulfills the commandments in faithfulness, accuracy and obedience, he will become a person whose heart is full of love to God and to others, as the Lord says; "If you keep My commandments, you will abide in My love, just as I have kept My Father's commandments and abide in His love. You are My friends if you do whatever I command you." (John 15:10,14), also; "But whoever keeps His word, truly the love of God is perfected in him. By this we know that we are in Him." (1 John 2:5), also; "Now he who keeps His commandments abides in Him, and He in him. And by this we know that He abides in us, by the Spirit whom He has given us." (1 John 3:24).

Keeping the commandments proves that we love the Lord, and we will then have favour in His eyes and our prayers will be accepted; "Now we know that God does not hear sinners; but if anyone is a worshiper of God and does His will, He hears him." (John 9:31); "For I have kept the ways of the

Lord, and have not wickedly departed from my God. For all His judgments were before me, and I did not put away His statutes from me. I was also blameless before Him, and I kept myself from my iniquity." (Psalm 18:21-23); "You have commanded us to keep Your precepts diligently." (Psalm 119:4); "Then Peter and the other apostles answered and said: We ought to obey God rather than men." (Acts 5:29. These quotations concern the commandments of dealings between people, or those who might be embarrassed to obey the commandments in front of people. As for the commandments regarding a persons own spiritual life, such as; fasting, prayer, alms giving, humility, etc., a monk has been ordained to struggle in order to perfect them, until he becomes a fifth Gospel; "You are our epistle written in our hearts, known and read by all men; you are manifestly an epistle of Christ, ministered by us, written not with ink but by the spirit of the living God, not on tablets of stone but on tablets of flesh, that is, of the heart" (2 Corinthians 3:2-3).

Dr Ragheb Abdul Nour in his book: 'St Anthony - A Church and a Spiritual Must', wrote; "When we study St Anthony's life, his asceticism and monastic teachings, we find they are all based on the Bible and obeying the commandments. At an early age and a son of a very rich family, St Anthony heard these words in the church, "Jesus said to him, 'If you want to be perfect, go, sell what you have and give to the poor, and you will have treasure in heaven; and come, follow Me.'" (Matthew 19:21). So he sold all his possessions, gave the money to the poor and just kept a little amount of money for his sister. Once more, he heard in the church, "Therefore do not worry about tomorrow, for tomorrow will worry about its own things. Sufficient for the day is its own trouble." (Matthew 6:34), so he went out and gave the rest to the poor, took his sister to a house of virgins (like a convent), then headed gradually into the inner wilderness, depending on the Lord, obeying all his commandments. In the wilderness, the commandments were his food and drink, obeying them and living in their light".

THE PLEASURE OF FULFILLING THE COMMANDMENTS

In the wilderness St Anthony found a good atmosphere, having solitude and serenity, to study the Holy Bible and meditate in its mysteries. He kept applying all the commandments with great wisdom and discernment, following the light of the commandments that led him to a perfect monastic life.

The father of monks found pleasure and comfort in fulfilling the commandments and felt the Divine support when fulfilling it faithfully and

20. Monasticism is a Life of Fulfilling the Commandments

accurately, according to the Lord's words; "It is the Spirit who gives life; the flesh profits nothing. The words that I speak to you are spirit, and they are life." (John 6:63); "And I know that His command is everlasting life. Therefore, whatever I speak, just as the Father has told Me, so I speak" (John 12:50); "for the word of God is living and powerful, and sharper than any two-edged sword, piercing even to the division of soul and spirit, and of joints and marrow, and is a discerner of the thoughts and intents of the heart." (Hebrews 4:12); "For the weapons of our warfare are not carnal but mighty in God for pulling down strongholds." (2 Corinthians 10:4), because the Lord has promised us; "I am ready to perform My word." (Jeremiah 1:12).

St Anthony's Gospel life was reflected in his monastic teachings to his disciples and children:

- "Wherever you go, consider the presence of God."
- "Every deed you do, have a verse from the Holy Bible as a witness for what you are doing."
- ""Rejoice in the Lord" means we rejoice in fulfilling the Lord's commandment."
- "All the commandments are not a burden, but they are true light and everlasting happiness to him who fulfils them."
- "If you are ordered to do things contradicting the Lord, remember that you ought to obey God more than people."
- "If you sit in your cell keep doing these things: Read the Holy Bible and Spiritual books, plead to God, do handwork."
- "Do not follow all your thoughts, but let your mind concentrate on the commandments at all times and how to perfect them."

Once, some brethren came to St Anthony asking; "Father, please tell us how to be saved." So he answered: "The Lord says 'whoever slaps you on your right cheek, turn the other to him also.'" They said: "We can't do this". So he said: "then tolerate the slap". They also said, "we can't". Finally, he called his disciple, asked him to prepare something for them to eat and then let them go because he considered them "sick people" who didn't like to follow the commandments.

The Children of St Anthony Followed his Footsteps:

His children used to love and study the Heavenly Commandments, and handed them down to their disciples, remembering the Lord's words; "Because narrow is the gate and difficult is the way which leads to life, and there are few who find it." (Matthew 7:24). Thus they gained the blessings that the Lord promised whoever follows His commandments; "Blessed is the man who walks not in the counsel of the ungodly, nor stands in the path of sinners, nor sits in the seat of the scornful but his delight is in the law of the Lord and in His law he meditates day and night." (Psalm 1:1-2).

"Blessed are those who keep justice, and he who does righteousness at all times!" (Psalm 106:3).

"Blessed are those who keep His testimonies, who seek Him with the whole heart! They also do no iniquity; They walk in His ways." (Psalm 119:2-3).

"Now therefore, listen to me, my children, for blessed are those who keep my ways. Hear instruction and be wise, and do not disdain it. Blessed is the man who listens to me, watching daily at my gates, waiting at the posts of my doors. For whoever finds me finds life, and obtains favour from the Lord; but he who sins against me wrongs his own soul; all those who hate me love death." (Proverbs 8:32-36).

"But He said; 'More than that, blessed are those who hear the word of God and keep it!'" (Luke 11:28).

"If you know these things, happy are you if you do them." (John 13:17).

"But he who looks into the perfect law of liberty and continues in it, and is not a forgetful hearer but a doer of the word, this one will be blessed in what he does." (James 1:25).

"Blessed is he who reads and those who hear the words of this prophecy and keep those things which are written in it; for the time is near." (Revelations 1:3).

"Blessed are those who do His commandments, that they may have the right to the tree of life, and may enter through the gates into the city." (Revelations 22:14).

The early fathers used to fully memorise the Holy Bible, for example, St Amonius who memorised both the Old and the New Testament; St Hiro, on his way to Scetis wilderness, memorised 15 Psalms, Psalm 119, the Book of Isaiah the Prophet, part of Jeremiah, St Luke's Gospel, Proverbs and the Epistle to the Hebrews.

THE BENEFITS OF KEEPING THE COMMANDMENTS

When the fathers kept the Commandments, consequently the Commandments preserved them. It made them great spiritual men, living a holy enlightened upright life according to the Lord's words; "My covenant was with him, one of life and peace, and I gave them to him that he might fear Me; so he feared Me and was reverent before My name." (Malachi 2:5).

It made them men of prayer of the highest level, landmarks on the way of spiritual struggle. Through their struggling and obtaining virtues it also made them men of miracles, able to cure diseases.

A Story from "The Paradise of The Holy Fathers", "A monk went to cast out a demon, as soon as he entered the house, the girl with the evil spirit came out and slapped him on the face, so the monk turned the other cheek, according to the commandment. Immediately the girl cried out and the demon departed from her screaming in pain and saying, "Woe to us because of Jesus' Commandments which hinder us continuously." Nothing so humiliates the pride of the devils except the humble fulfilment of the Lord Jesus' commandments."

21. Monasticism is a Life of Preparation for the Second Coming of the Lord Christ

Whenever the media announces a date for the second coming, people rush to the deserts, wilderness and mountains waiting for the awesome Second Coming of the Lord Jesus; "Then they will see the Son of Man coming in a cloud with power and great glory." (Luke 21:27), although no one knows that hour; "But of that day and hour no one knows, no, not even the angels of heaven, but My Father only." (Matthew 24:36).

Our concern here is that people know that the wilderness is the best place to get ready for the second coming, especially the monks, who totally believe in this fact, so they abandoned the whole world with its lust and headed towards the wilderness and mountains, spending their life in utmost repentance, preparing themselves to meet Lord Jesus without disgrace. They remember St Peter's words; "Therefore, since all these things will be dissolved, what manner of persons ought you to be in holy conduct and godliness, looking for and hastening the coming of the day of God, because of which the heavens will be dissolved being on fire, and the elements will melt with fervent heat? Nevertheless we, according to His promise, look for new heavens and a new earth in which righteousness dwells. Therefore, beloved, looking forward to these things, be diligent to be found by Him in peace, without spot and blameless." (2 Peter 3:11-14).

The saintly fathers also advised the monks to live their life in preparation of the second coming.

"A merchant while in the middle of the sea in his ship with his goods is always in fear, lest the storm would perish his goods, the same with the monk, as long as he is in the sea of this world, he is cautious lest any harm would attack him and destroy his life." St Isaac the Syrian

"Get ready to meet the Lord at any moment. Test yourself and discover where you fall short, so you avoid the horrible hour of death. Your brethren will see your good life and they will follow your steps." St Moses the Black

These saints spent all their lives as strangers in this world, looking forward to the Heavenly Jerusalem; "These all died in faith, not having received the promises, but having seen them afar off were assured of them, embraced them, and confessed that they were strangers and pilgrims on the earth. For those who say such things declare plainly that they seek a homeland. And truly if they had called to mind that country from which they had come out, they would have had opportunity to return. But now they desire a better, that is, a heavenly country. Therefore God is not ashamed to be called their God, for he has prepared a city for them." "They were stoned, they were sawn in two, were tempted, were slain with the sword. They wandered about in sheepskins and goatskins, being destitute, afflicted, tormented – of whom the world was not worthy. They wandered in deserts and mountains, in dens and caves of the earth." (Hebrews 11: 13-16, 37-38).

St Arsenius was always conscious of his departure. At the hour of his departure he said to his disciples; "the fear of this hour has accompanied me since I became a monk." He departed with tears falling from his eyes, which he always had, while the monks kept crying and kissing his feet, farwelling him as a stranger who finally reached his home town. Pope Theophilus, at the time of the saints departure said; "Blessed are you St Arsenius, you wept all the days of your life waiting for this hour."

One of the saints said; "I imagine the angels descending and ascending every moment taking souls, and I expect my departure at any moment, saying with the Psalmist, 'My heart is steadfast, O God, my heart is steadfast; I will sing and give praise.' (Psalm 57:7)."

Mother Sarah used to live in readiness of her departure at all times, she used to say; "When I am going upstairs, I put one foot on the stairs and expect death before lifting up the other foot."

A person who expects death at any moment, always considers today as his last day in life, so he tries to make it an ideal, perfect day in behaviour, prayers and all the other spiritual practices, trying to avoid all sins and living in continuous repentance. In monasticism, a monk is always repeating this wonderful verse; "Amen, Even so, come, Lord Jesus" (Revelation 22:21).

Getting Ready for the Second Coming in the World as Compared to in the Wilderness

In the world the responsibilities and concerns increase as we grow up, and we become very busy. The Bible says; "Remember now your Creator in the days of your youth, before the difficult days come and the years draw near when you say, 'I have no pleasure in them.'" (Ecclesiastes 12:1). But for the monk it is completely different, the more he gets older, the closer he comes to God and further he goes from the busy world. His only concern becomes praying and meditating in the Heavenly matters, getting ready for eternity.

We are now so close to the second coming, according to all the signs that Lord Jesus mentioned, so we need to live a true life of repentance and watchfulness; "Therefore thus will I do to you, O Israel; and because I will do this to you, prepare to meet your God, O Israel." (Amos 4:12), "not forsaking the assembling of ourselves together, as is the manner of some, but exhorting one another, and so much the more as you see the Day approaching." (Hebrews 10:25). Also; "But the end of all things is at hand; therefore be serious and watchful in your prayers." (1 Peter 4:7), and; "You also be patient. Establish your hearts, for the coming of the Lord is at hand." (James 5:8).

The Wisdom of this Age

Let us take the wisdom of this age as a useful lesson for our spiritual life. A student doubles his effort when the exams come closer in order to attain a pass with credit or distinction. A sailor in the sea prepares to reach the port safely as soon as he sees his ship coming close to the shore. As for us, we are waiting for the Final Judgment, where the Lord will reward each one according to his deeds. In heaven the Lord Jesus Christ, the angels and the saints are waiting for us to be saved from the troubles of this world. Let us cry out with rejoicing; "My heart is steadfast, O God, my heart is steadfast; I will sing and give praise." (Psalm 57:7), and, "Amen, Even so, come Lord Jesus!" (Revelation 22:20).

Our wonderful church has prepared the readings of 22 Tubah, the commemoration of the departure of St Anthony to be from Luke 12:35-40, where it talks about getting ready for the Second Coming; "Let your waist be girded and your lamps burning; and you yourselves be like men who wait for their master, when he will return from the wedding, that when he comes and knocks they may open to him immediately. Blessed are those servants whom the master, when he comes, will find watching. Assuredly, I say to you that he will gird himself and have them sit down to eat, and will come and serve them. And if he should come in the second watch, or come in the third watch, and find them so, blessed are those servants. But know this, that if the master of the house had known what hour the thief would come, he would have watched and not allowed his house to be broken into. Therefore you also be ready, for the Son of Man is coming at an hour you do not expect." (Luke 12:35-40).

22. Monasticism is an Angelic Life and a Heavenly Rite

Our Lord Jesus said to the Sadducees; "But those who are counted worthy to attain that age, and the resurrection from the dead, neither marry nor are given in marriage; nor can they die anymore, for they are equal to the angels and are sons of God, being sons of the resurrection." (Luke 20:35-36). Also; "For when they rise from the dead, they neither marry nor are given in marriage, but are like angels in heaven." (Mark 12:25). The monks in monasteries live an angelic life; they do not care about worldly matters, they just concentrate on praying and praising God. In the monastery a monk lives celibate, thus freeing himself of all the worries and responsibilities of a married person and so the divine words; "For when they rise from the dead, they neither marry nor are given in marriage, but are like angels in heaven." (Mark 12:25), apply to them. They follow the rite of the angels in praising the Lord at all times saying; "Holy, Holy, Holy, O Lord of Hosts heaven and earth are full of Your Holy Glory" and hence they fulfill the words mentioned in the Liturgy of St Gregory; "He who gave those on earth the praise of the Seraphim." The monks are considered earthly angels and heavenly human beings.

The early fathers said; "As much as a monk is eager to be with God all the time without frivolity, likewise the Grace of God will be doubled on Him. The more we get closer to God, the more He cares for us".

St Anthony said; "He who is dwelling in the wilderness has avoided three fights, those that emerge from sight, hearing and talking." A monk who preserves his celibacy without blemish, becomes a pure censer from which comes a sweet aroma of incense, thus the Lord will accept his prayers and asceticism.

The early fathers frequently reminded the monks of their angelic rank.

"A monk is like an angel, he should not abandon the work of the heavenliness, for the sake of vain glory and righteousness in the world." St Isaac the Syrian

St Macarius the Great rebuked some monks for their reluctance; "Because of our reluctance, we became laymen, not having the angelic rite anymore. Ask my brethren: do angels collect money and worship God? When we put on these clothes, was it to collect possessions for ourselves or to become like angels?"

"Let your body be illuminated with purity like the Seraphim. Let your soul be free from pains and thoughts like them. They are ablazing with fire due to their being in the presence of God at all times." St John Saba

23. Monasticism is a Life of Spiritual Happiness

Christianity is the religion of true happiness and joy, and the New Testament is the most joyful Book in the whole world. It starts with the joy of the Birth of our Lord Jesus and ends with the wonderful picture of the hosts of saints singing joyfully, "Alleluia".

Even in his farewell address to His disciples, the Lord says; "These things I have spoken to you, that My joy may remain in you, and that your joy may be full" (John 15:11). When He ascended to heaven; "So continuing daily with one accord in the temple, and breaking bread from house to house, they ate their food with gladness and simplicity of heart" (Acts 2:46). While they were beaten; "So they departed from the presence of the council, rejoicing that they were counted worthy to suffer shame for His name" (Acts 5:41), in jail; "But at midnight Paul and Silas were praying and singing hymns to God, and the prisoners were listening to them." (Acts 16:25), and there are many other examples of rejoicing.

Peace is the inner stability of the soul in spite of the pains and temptations. It is the sweetest feeling, the pinnacle of happiness, and it is perfection. Peace is the precious inheritance, which our Lord Jesus left for us after His ascension; "Peace I leave with you, My peace I give to you; not as the world gives do I give to you. Let not your heart be troubled, neither let it be afraid." (John 14:27). He also comforted us saying; "These things I have spoken to you, that in Me you may have peace. In the world you will have tribulation; but be of good cheer, I have overcome the world." (John 16:33).

MONASTICISM IS THE SUMMIT OF CHRISTIAN HAPPINESS

A Christian layman may lose his inner peace and joy because of the world's tribulations, yet a monk in the wilderness is away from these disturbing circumstances. At a first glimpse, monasticism looks like a life of grief, struggle, sadness and tears. A monk willingly deprives himself of the pleasures of this world, living in the dry desert, wearing black for the rest of his life. Although this is true, this does not lessen the fact that monasticism is a life of inner joy and that the monk is the happiest person on earth; "Though now you do not see Him, yet believing, you rejoice with joy inexpressible and full of glory." (1 Peter 1:8). The life of a monk is like the Tabernacle that Moses established in the wilderness; "Then he made a covering for the tent of rams' skins dyed red, and a covering of badger skins above that." (Exodus 36:19) It looks ugly from outside, but so beautiful from inside; "The royal daughter is all glorious within the palace; her clothing is woven with gold." (Psalm 45:13).

REASONS FOR THE DEEP SPIRITUAL JOY OF MONKS

1. Celibacy: A married person continually worries about his family and children and sometimes it is a life of grief and shame if a married couple have no children. For example, Rachael, when she didn't have children said to Jacob, "Here is my maid Bilhah, go in to her, and she will bear a child on my knees that I also may have children by her.'" (Genesis 30:3). Hannah, Samuel's mother; "and her rival also provoked her severely, to make her miserable, because the Lord had closed her womb." (1 Samuel 1:6). When Elizabeth fell pregnant, she said; "Thus the Lord has dealt with me, in the days when He looked on me, to take away my reproach among men". (Luke 1:25).

Not only women grieve for not having children but also men, we see Abraham the father of fathers, when Sarah his wife was barren, the Lord said to him; "Do not be afraid, Abram, I am your shield, your exceedingly great reward.' But Abram said, 'Lord God, what will You give me, seeing I go childless, and the heir of my house is Eliezer of Damascus?' Then Abram said, 'Look, You have given me no offspring; indeed one born in my house is my heir!'" (Genesis 15:1-3). Abraham was not comforted until he heard the Lord's promise; "And behold, the word of the Lord came to him, saying, 'This one shall not be your heir, but one who will come from your own body shall be your heir.' Then He brought him outside and said, 'Look now toward heaven, and count the stars if you are able to number them.' And He said to him, 'so shall your descendants be.' And he believed in the Lord, and He accounted it to him for righteousness. Then He said to him, 'I am the Lord, who brought you out of Ur of the Chaldeans, to give you this land to inherit it.'" (Genesis 15:4-7).

But as for a monk his children are his struggles in gaining virtues. St Gregory of Nyssa praised celibacy saying; "Celibacy is a fortress against all pains. In celibacy no one becomes a widow because they are always in the presence of the Everlasting Groom. Its children are completely consecrated. Its house is always ornamented with riches because the Lord Christ Himself is dwelling there. So, separation will never occur but rather unity with Whom the soul is yearning to, as the Apostle says: "For I am hard pressed between the two, having a desire to depart and be with Christ, which is far better." (Philippians 1:23)."

2. Pilgrimage: Monasticism is a life of pilgrimage being separated from family, relatives and friends, for the sake of communion with the One. It is an eternal partnership; "Therefore, from now on, we regard no one according to the flesh. Even though we have known Christ according to the flesh, yet now we know Him thus no longer." (2 Corinthians 5:16). The monk's mother is St Mary and His Father is the Lord Jesus. A monk never grieves for the death of a wife or children.

The Spiritual Family of a Monk - St John Climacus names the family of a monk:

Father: He whoever helps and supports you when you sin.

Mother: Ascetism that cleanses your sins.

Brother: He who struggles with you to lift you up to perfection.

Wife: The continuous remembrance of death (a wife that you can never abandon).

Children: The sighs of your heart.

Slave: Your body.

Friends: The powers that can save you at the time of the departure of your soul.

3. Fulfilling the Commandment Accurately: The monk who follows the commandments honestly and accurately will feel the blessings of its fullfilment as well as God's Hand and support. Thus he will be happy and will rejoice all the days of his life; "Blessed are the undefiled in the way, who walk in the law of the Lord! Blessed are those who keep His testimonies, who seek Him with the whole heart!" (Psalm 119:1-2). Once St Anthony was asked what did the apostle mean when he said, "Rejoice in the Lord." So he answered; "If we fulfil the commandment we will rejoice, that is the joy of the Lord and we also rejoice for the success of our brethren who are doing the same. Let us preserve ourselves from the joy and laughter of the vain world, if we really want to be the children of God."

4. A Clear Conscience: A monk who is doing the right thing, following the right path, will feel the joy of a clear and peaceful conscience, always trying to follow in the footsteps of the great saints of the church like St Anthony, St Macarius, St Pachomius, St Shenouda and many others. The wilderness will then become a place of peace, comfort and joy, as the Psalmist says; "Both the singers and the players on instruments say, all my springs are in you" (Psalm 87:7); and; "I have blotted out, like a thick cloud, your transgressions, and like a cloud, your sings. Return to Me, for I have redeemed you." (Isaiah 44:22).

5. The Life of Poverty: Every single person in the world has his own troubles and worries whether he is the king of the city or the poorest person because; "Yet man is born to trouble, as the sparks fly upward." (Job 5:7). But as for the monk who is living a life of chosen poverty, he feels great joy and peace, as it is written; "Better is a dry morsel with quietness, than a house full of feasting with strife." (Proverbs 17:1); also; "You have put gladness in my heart, more than in the season that their grain and wine increased." (Psalm 4:7).

He who has many possessions and properties will always be worried and busy with his wealth. But a monk never regrets the loss of anything, his interests are not in collecting money or other possessions, he is trying to fulfil the Lord's words; "For all these things the nations of the world seek after, and your Father knows that you need these things. But seek the kingdom of God, and all these things shall be added to you." (Luke

12: 30-31). Also the apostle's words; "and having food and clothing, with these we shall be content." (1 Timothy 6:8).

The early monks lived just like birds who are flying on the wings of faith, depending only on God Who looks after them as He promised; "I will give you the treasures of darkness and hidden riches of secret places, that you may know that I, the Lord, who call you by your name am the God of Israel." (Isaiah 45:3).

6. The Life of Purity: A monk is always trying to keep his heart clean and pure in order to be a dwelling place for Christ the King, thus his heart will be over-filled with peace and joy. If a monk, by God's Grace, gets rid of the following temptations, he will live in continuous unutterable joy:

- The pain and temptation of being greedy for food and drink. Through fasting, a monk learns moderation in his eating habits which will aid him to perform his spiritual practices and will add to his joy.

- The pain and temptation of sexual desires; a monk will live in purity offering his body as an acceptable pure sacrifice.

- The pain and temptation of acquiring possessions; a monk will live free on earth, feeling more pleasure in giving than in taking. He will store all his riches in heaven, where there are no robbers, no rust or moths.

- The pain and temptation of vice and anger, which is the father of madness; a monk will become a peaceful and meek person resembling his Master, loved by everyone. He will live in peace with himself and those around him.

- The pain and temptation of the human ego; a monk will love his brethren and wish them the best. His heart will become a source of peace and joy.

THE ACCEPTABLE PRAYER

A monk who is overcoming temptations and meticulously keeps the commandments will have great favour in Gods eyes during his prayers, as the Apostle says; "And whatever we ask we received from Him, because we keep His commandments and do those things that are pleasing in His sight." (1 John 3:22). Also as the Lord promises; "Until now you have asked nothing in

My name, Ask, and you will receive, that your joy may be full." (John 16:24). Feeling that the Lord is accepting his prayer will add to the joy of a monk; he will live heaven on earth, a life of thanksgiving and faith, repeating with the Psalmist; "Make a joyful shout to the Lord, all you lands! Serve the Lord with gladness; come before His presence with singing. Know that the Lord, he is God; It is He who has made us, and not we ourselves; We are His people and the sheep of His pasture. Enter into His gates with thanksgiving, and into His courts with praise. Be thankful to Him, and bless His name. For the Lord is good; His mercy is everlasting, and His truth endures to all generations." (Psalm 100:1-5).

St John Chrysostom talks beautifully about the life of peace and joy that the monks enjoy: "Those monks who are always meditating in the heavenly Kingdom and in continuous communion with God, their cells and caves are quiet, their bodies are void of pains, they are more pure than the light. Their job is as that of Adam before his fall, that is, talking to God freely, living in the Paradise that is full of blessings and happiness. They are not less than Adam, they even may have more blessings because of the great grace poured on them through the Holy Spirit. Like the angels, in one happy heart and voice, as if it is coming out of one mouth, they praise the Lord, honour and thank Him."

24. The Basic Fundamentals of Monasticism

The monk is a person who wants to follow the Lord with all his heart, denying himself and carrying his cross daily in the path of Golgotha, with all its long-sufferings and pains. There, he crucifies himself willingly and happily with Jesus Christ; "But God forbid that I should glory except in the cross of our Lord Jesus Christ, by whom the world has been crucified to me, and I to the world." (Galatians 6:14), and; "I have been crucified with Christ; it is no longer I who live, but Christ lives in me; and the life which I now live in the flesh I live by faith in the Son of God, who loved me and gave Himself for me" (Galatians 2:20).

The reason for the monk's delight in the Cross is his feeling that he is fulfilling the command of his Master; "And when He had called the people to Him, with His disciples also, He said to them, 'Whoever desires to come after me, let him deny himself, and take up his cross, and follow Me'". (Mark 8:34), and, "Enter by the narrow gate; for wide is the gate and broad is the way that leads to destruction, and there are many who go in by it." (Matthew 7:13).

The Cross is also connected to the Resurrection. Had it not been for the cross and its sufferings, there could not have been a Resurrection, Ascension and the Lord Jesus sitting on the right of the Father.

St Paphnutius (one of the 4th century fathers) advised a novice monk; "Abandoning the world is the proof of dying to it and carrying the Cross, so you have to know that you already died to all the desires and lust of the world, as the Apostle says, "But God forbid that I should glory except in the cross of our Lord Jesus Christ, by whom the world has been crucified to me, and I to the world." (Galatians 6:14). From now on, "I have been crucified with Christ; it is no longer I who live, but Christ lives in me; and the life which I now live in the flesh I live by faith in the Son of God, who loved me and gave Himself for me" (Galatians 2:20). You have to get ready, "This is the gate of the Lord, through which the righteous shall enter." (Psalm 118:20)."

Now you might ask: How could a person carry his cross at all times? Or how could a living person crucify himself? The answer is: the fear of God is our Cross, so, a crucified person cannot move any of his body parts freely to any direction; so we have to fix our desires and wishes not on what pleases us, but according to God's commandments.

Three nails are on the cross by which a monk is living:

I. Chastity

II. Obedience

III. Poverty

By these three nails he is crucifying three major sins; "For all that is in the world – the lust of the flesh, the lust of the eyes, and the pride of life – is not of the Father but is of the world" (1 John 2:16).

We know that the Lord Jesus did not die immediately after being hung on the Cross, he kept struggling and suffering for three hours and then finally he submitted His Soul. It is the same for a monk, his desires will not die at once as soon as he is ordained a monk, but he keeps struggling and fighting while being crucified on the Cross of ascetism, purity and struggle. His desires will fade away bit by bit until they die completely with the Grace of God.

I. CHASTITY

Chastity in monasticism means refraining from any sexual desire out of extreme love for Jesus Christ. This love is the secret of the ability to overcome the bodily desires.

Christian chastity is deep; it goes to the extent of chastity in behaviour and thoughts as well as the body. The love of the Lord is the thing that inflames the heart with the love of chastity. It calms down the body. Chastity is one of the works of the Holy Spirit in the person who wants to live with Christ.

One of the Holy Liturgy Fractions says; "Master Christ is the Teacher of Chastity, the establisher of everlasting acceptable pure prayers".

The Psalmist says; "With the pure You will show Yourself pure; and with the devious you will show Yourself shrewd" (Psalm 18:26), which means that God helps a person who seeks perfection, or who seeks purity etc.

Monasticism, as a great path of salvation, includes celibates and virgins who were happy and content to have Christ as the Groom of their souls. They offered their virginity as a sacrifice of love, on the altar of chastity and consecration.

Monasticism also includes the widows who never re-married and offered the rest of their lives to the Lord, clinging to Him, not being interested in another relationship. Sometimes a married couple mutually consent for the husband to go to a monastery and the wife go to a convent. Like St John Kame, St Ammoun the father of Nitria mountain, St Andronikos and his wife Anastasia and many others.

The path of virginity is the greatest way to heaven, for God created the angels with intellect but without the desire; He created the animals with the desire but not the intellect and he created man with intellect and desire. If the desire conquers the intellect, a man becomes like an animal but if the intellect conquers the desire then he becomes like an angel. He who keeps his chastity and purity struggling till the end, will definitely join the 144,000 celibates in heaven, whom St John the Disciple saw; "Then I looked, and behold, a Lamb standing on Mount Zion, and with Him one hundred and forty-four thousand, having His Father's name written on their foreheads. And I heard a voice from heaven, like the voice of many waters, and like the voice of loud thunder. And I heard the sound of harpists playing their harps. And they sang as it were a new song before the throne, before the four living creatures and the elders; and no one could learn that song except the hundred and forty-four thousand who were redeemed from the earth. These are the ones who were not defiled with women, for they are virgins. These are the ones who follow the Lamb wherever He goes. These were redeemed from among men being first fruits to God and to the Lamb. And in their mouth was found no guile, for they are without fault before the throne of God." (Revelations 14:1-5).

The Fathers' Sayings About Chastity and Virginity

"He who is reluctant in his chastity will be ashamed when standing for prayers." St Moses the Black.

"God requests three things of those who are baptised:

1. Upright Faith

2. Honesty of the Tongue

3. Purity and Chastity of the Body." St Gregory the Theologian. Here, the saint places purity and chastity as important as faith.

"Rich people watch out lest someone would come and steal their treasures, so what about us, we also have to watch lest the devil should come and steal the goodness that we have achieved because of our chastity and purity." One of the saints.

Some examples of saints struggling for chastity

Many saints preferred to lose their lives or parts of their bodies than to lose their chastity.

One of the monks was suffering from the fight of adultery, so he left his cell and went to a hyena's cave saying; "It is better for me to be killed by this hyena than to be killed by sin." He stayed there for six days fasting, on the seventh day, the hyena got him some food. He kept living in this cave for 40 days, during which the hyena was getting him food. Finally, he heard a voice saying to him "Be Strong", after which the fight of adultery departed from him and he, thanking God, returned to his cell.

A nun was captured by one of the soldiers who wanted to sin with her but she told him to wait because she knew a secret which could protect him as he was a soldier and in continuous threat of death during wars. She said to him, "I have some oil, if you anoint yourself with it and get hit by any weapon, it will never hurt you. Now, let me anoint your neck and give me your sword and you will see it won't hurt you." The soldier said, "No, let me try this oil on you first". So she answered "OK, anoint my neck, and with your full strength hit my throat with your sword". When he did so, her head was cut off immediately and the soldier grieved that he killed such an innocent beautiful nun.

Another saint bit off his tongue and spat it in the face of a prostitute who wanted to make him sin with her while his hands and legs were tied.

We should be proud of celibacy remembering that St Mary is the Ever Virgin after giving birth to our Lord Jesus, as we call her in the praise, "The Virgin the Pride of Virginity".

II. Obedience

Obedience is the inner listening to the voice of God and the spiritual guide of confession, who is guiding us for the sake of our spiritual benefit and salvation. The Apostle advises us; "Children, obey your parents in the Lord, for this is right." (Ephesians 6:1), and; "Now with whom was He angry forty years? Was it not with those who sinned, whose corpses fell in the wilderness?" (Hebrews 3:17).

Obedience in monasticism is the second nail with which a monk crucifies his personal will and desires as St John Climacus says; "Obedience is burying your will."

In the rites of ordination, a monk does the following:

1. Bows in a metania in front of the altar to show obedience and submission to God and the church.

2. A metania to the Abbot in obedience to the monastery and its rules and life style.

3. A metania to all the monks, then he goes to them individually asking their absolution and that they would accept his monasticism.

From the commandments read at the end of the rites of ordination, it says; "You have to have perfect submission and obedience. Listen to him who is guiding you towards the path of God and His Holy commandments, so that you might gain the crown of the children of God and inherit the heavenly Kingdom with all the saints who pleased God ever since the beginning."

A monk should submit his human will into the hands of the Divine will saying; "Father, if it is Your will, remove this cup from me; nevertheless not My will, but Yours, be done." (Luke 22:42).

It is a common rule for a monk to build his monastic life on a solid base of virtues. He has to submit his will to his spiritual father and his brethrens' will. The tests of obedience which the early fathers had given to their children are not easily accepted by anyone, yet they were designed to teach a monk how to give up his own will, in order to be lifted up to a certain level of perfection.

St John Cassian says; "The novice monks used to act quickly on what they were ordered to do, as if it is an order descending from heaven. They even accepted impossible matters, in faith and awe, and did their best to complete the order. In their cells, if anyone knocks on the door, they hurried and opened and listened carefully, even if they were in the middle of writing a word they hurry to open the door without finishing the word (like Mark the disciple of St Selwane). The fathers considered the virtue of obedience more important than handwork, reading, silence or any other virtue. The early fathers taught the monks not to hide any bad thoughts, but rather disclose them to their spiritual father, so that he could guide and instruct them because hiding and keeping these thoughts might make their heart a dwelling of satanic thoughts. Many times the Lord blessed the disciple monks because of their total obedience and we will mention just two incidents as examples:

St Pambo gave a wooden rod to his disciple St. John the Short asking him to plant it and water it daily. St John obeyed even though he had to walk for miles daily to get water. In order to get the water, St John would start walking at night and coming back the next morning. After three years the wooden rod became a tree with fruits. St John brought some of these fruits to St Pambo who took them to the brethren and said, "Eat from the fruits of obedience."

A saint asked his disciple to get him an old jar from near the cemetery. A hyena was dwelling at this cemetery. When the disciple asked "what about the hyena, father", the saint answered "tie it and bring it to me". The disciple went and when the hyena saw him, it ran away, yet the disciple said, "My father ordered me to tie you and take you back to him." So the hyena obeyed. When the elder saint saw his disciple coming with the hyena, he was astonished at his great obedience but lest the disciple should fall in vain glory, he said to this him, "I asked you for the hyena not a dog!" Then he untied the hyena and let it go.

Some of the Fathers' sayings about Obedience

"Do not be at ease, lest you become a pot for all evils. Listen to your father then you will have the blessing of the Lord." St Anthony

"Obedience and humility will submit beasts under our feet." St Anthony

"Those who live without guidance will fall off like the leaves of a tree, because they ignored the commandment, "Remember the days of old, consider the years of many generations. Ask your father, and he will show you; Your elders, and they will tell you." (Deuteronomy 32:7)". St Anthony

"Listen my son and accept instruction. Love him who is guiding you in God's fear. Be obedient like Isaac who listened to his father as a naive lamb." St Pachomius the Father of Kononia (Community)

"Obedience is the pride of a monk, God will listen to the prayers of he who acquires it, he will be standing before the Crucified, the Lord of Glory Himself because our Lord Jesus was crucified for us out of his obedience to His Father." St Adrias

"Obedience is sailing in the sea safely without any danger." St John Climacus

"Obedience is like a person swimming in the sea, carried by another one who is an expert in swimming, and hence they will both reach the shore safely." St John Climacus

"Obedience is life, disobedience is death." St Orisius, one of the followers of St Pachomius

By Being Obedient, You are Imitating Jesus Christ

It is a great pride that whoever practices obedience imitates our Lord Jesus, Who obeyed His Father till death as He said; "My food is to do the will of him who sent me, and to finish His work." (John 4:34). "I speak what I have seen with My Father" (John 8:38). "But that the world may know that I love the Father, and as the Father gave Me commandment, so I do. Arise, let us go from here." (John 14:31). "Father, if it is Your will, remove this cup from Me; nevertheless not My will but Yours, be done" (Luke 22:42).

St Paul the Apostle advises us to imitate Jesus in His obedience; "Let each of you look out not only for his own interests, but also for the interests of others. Let this mind be in you which was also in Christ Jesus, who, being in the form of God, did not consider it robbery to be equal with God, but made Himself of no reputation, taking the form of a servant, and coming in the likeness of men. And being found in appearance as a man, He humbled Himself and became obedient to the point of death, even the death of the cross. Therefore God also has highly exalted Him and given Him the name which is above every name, that at the name of Jesus every knee should bow, of those in heaven, and of those on earth, and of those under the earth, and that every tongue should confess that Jesus Christ is Lord, to the glory of God the Father." (Philippians 2:4-11), and; "having been perfected, He became the author of eternal salvation to all who obey Him." (Hebrews 5:9).

The Blessings of Obedience to the Guide

"Obedience quenches all the hot arrows of the enemy." One of the fathers

A story written in the "Paradise of The Holy Fathers": A father took his baby son and went to the wilderness where the son grew up and was ordained as a monk. After a while the devils started to tempt him with the sin of adultery, so he said to his father: "I am going back to the world, I cannot resist this harsh fight." The father calmed him down and instructed him not to leave his monastic vow. Finally, the father asked him to take 80 pieces of bread and some palm branches, sufficient for 40 days of braiding baskets, and to go into the inner wilderness. The son did so, and after 20 days, the devil, who used to fight him, appeared to him in a horrible sight, having a rotten smell. When the monk started dismissing it, the devil said, "Why are you dismissing me now? Didn't you desire me eagerly at a certain time? Yet, because you have obeyed your father, God saved you from me." The monk thanked the Lord and returned to his father. After he told his father what happened, his father said, "If you would have waited till the end of the 40 days as I instructed you, you would have seen something greater than that."

Truly, the devil with all his tricks and fights cannot deceive a person who is obeying his father's advice and not acting according to his own will, as it is written; "Two are better than one, because they have a good reward for their labour, for if they fall, one will lift up his companion. But woe to him who is alone when he falls for he has no one to help him up." (Ecclesiastes 4:9-10), also; "Where there is no counsel, the people fall; but in the multitude of counsellors there is safety." (Proverbs 11:14).

The Limits of Obeying the Guide

Obedience should be in wisdom and understanding because it is to God first, then to man. If these 2 kinds of obedience clash, then we should listen to St Peter's saying; "We ought to obey God rather than man." (Acts 5:29), also; "Children, obey your parents in the Lord, for this is right" (Ephesians 6:1).

Obedience should be "in the Lord", the guide is only like the good shepherd who is guiding his disciples in the fields of the Divine Commandment, leading them to the source of Biblical living waters, helping them to discover their inner potential and benefit from them.

24. The Basic Fundamentals of Monasticism

St Paul explains the limits of authority in parenthood and priesthood; "For we can do nothing against the truth, but for the truth. Therefore I write these things being absent, lest being present I should use sharpness, according to the authority which the Lord has given me for edification and not for destruction." (2 Corinthians 13:8, 10).

If you are not convinced or comfortable about what your guide has told you, discuss it with him in love in order that both of you reach, with the Grace of God, an acceptable decision.

How can a monk live a life of obedience?

1. Humility: A humble person always leans towards obedience. St Anthony once saw the traps of the devil spread everywhere, so he prayed and asked God "who can escape all these traps?", a voice came from heaven saying "the humble one will escape them". A humble person respects other opinions, as long as they are sensible, even if they are different than his. We all know that man by his nature yearns to evil, he always protects and defends himself, even though he is wrong, as the Prophet says; "The heart is deceitful above all things, and desperately wicked; who can know it?" (Jeremiah 17:9), also; "not that we are sufficient of ourselves to think of anything as being from ourselves, but our sufficiency is from God" (2 Corinthians 3:5). So let us listen to his advice; "Be of the same mind toward one another. Do not set your mind on high things, but associate with the humble. Do not be wise in your own opinion." (Romans 12:16), and; "Well said, because of unbelief they were broken off, and you stand by faith. Do not be haughty, but fear." (Romans 11:20).

2. Repentance: A person who is living the life of repentance wants to be obedient, considering his past evil deeds a lesson not to depend on his personal wisdom and desires. Thus, he listens to his spiritual guide, "that he no longer should live the rest of his time in the flesh for the lusts of men, but for the will of God" (1 Peter 4:2).

3. Completely Abandoning Our Own Desire: We can obtain the life of obedience if we willingly abandon our own desires and will for the sake of God, knowing that he who follows his own will without guidance or instruction will lose his way and become a target for the devil's attacks.

Saul the king is an example of fulfilling his own will, when he didn't listen to Samuel the Prophet. He offered the sacrifice on his own, not waiting for Samuel. God immediately rejected him, the Spirit of the Lord departed from him and an evil spirit entered him.

Let us listen to Samuel the Prophet; "Then Samuel said: 'has the Lord as great delight in burnt offerings and sacrifices, as in obeying the voice of the Lord? Behold, to obey is better than sacrifice, and to heed than the fat of rams. For rebellion is as the sin of witchcraft, and stubbornness is as iniquity and idolatry. Because you have rejected the word of the Lord. He also has rejected you from being king.'" (1 Samuel 15;22-23), also, "Sacrifice and offering You did not desire; my ears You have opened; burnt offering and sin offering You did not require, then I said 'Behold I come; in the scroll of the Book it is written of me. I delight to do Your will, O my God, and Your law is within my heart.'" (Psalm 40:6-8).

4. Faith and Trust in the Spiritual Father and His Love: Have faith and trust in your spiritual father, as a person responsible for your salvation. He is a true father who is concerned for your spiritual prosperity, whom you can easily obey and disclose all your inner thoughts, following the Lord's commandment; "And if a son of peace is there, your peace will rest on it; if not, it will return to you." (Luke 10:6).

A monk should always pray for his spiritual father, so that God might give him wisdom in guiding others.

III. Poverty

Voluntary poverty is the token of eternal life, a life of meditation and continual union with God, without worry for belongings or possessions, as the Lord teaches; "If you want to be perfect, go sell what you have and give to the poor and you will have treasure in heaven, and come follow Me" (Matthew 19:21).

Listen to St Paul; "But what things were gain to me, these I have counted loss for Christ, but indeed I also count all things loss for the excellence of the knowledge of Christ Jesus my Lord, for whom I have suffered the loss of all things, and count them as rubbish, that I may gain Christ." (Philippians 3:7-9); "Not that I speak in regard to need, for I have learned in whatever state I am to be content." (Philippians 4:11), and; "And everyone who has left houses or brothers or sisters or father or mother or wife or children or lands for My name's sake, shall receive a hundredfold and inherit everlasting life." (Matthew 19:29).

24. The Basic Fundamentals of Monasticism

The early fathers were meticulous in making sure that the novice monk had willingly abandoned his possessions, job and all the belongings of the world, keeping only the Cross of the Lord Jesus Christ the Greatest Teacher. It is considered a great sin if someone in the monastery says 'my book' or 'my pen'.

A monk who abandons everything resembles our Master Jesus Christ; "and Jesus said to him, foxes have holes and birds of the air have nests, but the Son of man has nowhere to lay His head" (Matthew 8:20). He also resembles the pure Apostles in the early church; "For to this you were called, because Christ also suffered for us, leaving us an example, that you should follow His steps." (1 Peter 2:21), and St Paul; "Do you not know that you are the temple of God and that the Spirit of God dwells in you?" (1 Corinthians 2:16). At the beginning of the Disciples service, when Jesus called them; "So when they had brought their boats to land, they forsook all and followed Him." (Luke 5:11).

They left all the vain possessions to enjoy the eternal life, a living example of voluntary poverty. St Peter and St John were going to pray, when a lame man asked them for alms; "And fixing his eyes on him, with John, Peter said, "Look at us" So he gave them his attention, expecting to receive something from them. Then Peter said, "Silver and gold I do not have, but what I do have I give you: In the name of Jesus Christ of Nazareth, rise up and walk." And he took him by the right hand and lifted him up, and immediately his feet and ankle bones received strength. So he, leaping up, stood and walked and entered the temple with them, walking, leaping, and praising God." (Acts 3:4-8).

St Paul describes his state in 2 Corinthians 6:9-10; "as unknown, and yet well known; as dying, and behold we live; as chastened, and yet not killed; as sorrowful, yet always rejoicing; as poor, yet making many rich; as having nothing, and yet possessing all things."

The first church also lived in unity and voluntary poverty; "Now the multitude of those who believed were of one heart and one soul; neither did anyone say that any of the things he possessed was his own, but they had all things in common." (Acts 4:32).

25. Nothing is Greater Than Monasticism

A story from "The Paradise of The Holy Fathers":

"Once a priest of the idols came to St Macarius bowing and saying, "For the sake of the love of Jesus Christ, baptise me and ordain me as a monk". St Macarius was astonished and asked him, "Tell me, how did you come to Jesus Christ without preaching?" He answered: "We had a great celebration for the idols, after we finished everything; I slept inside one of the idols' altars. I saw a great king, surrounded by lots of counsellors and nobles, then one of his servants came, so the king asked him, 'where did you return from?' he answered, 'from this certain country, and I did a great job. I put in the heart of a woman some murmuring words told by a friend about her and so the women started fighting, then the husbands joined them and so on till lots of people were killed.' But the king did not like this and said, 'You've done nothing worthwhile. Go away!' Many other devils came telling their horrible stories, but none of them pleased the king. At the end one of them came and said to the king: 'I came from the Scetis wilderness. I have been fighting one monk for 40 years and today, finally, he fell in the sin, so I came quickly to tell you.' Here the king was overjoyed and praised him, he took off his crown and put it on his head and made him sit on the king's throne, saying, 'Truly, you have done a great deed today, congratulations.'" The priest then said, "When I saw all of this from my hiding place, I told myself there is nothing greater than monasticism and came to you." St Macarius baptised and ordained him, and he became one of the most honourable fathers in the wilderness."

The Lord commands us; "Therefore you shall be perfect, just as your Father in heaven is perfect." (Matthew 5:48) and monasticism helps a person to achieve the summit of Biblical perfection.

CPSIA information can be obtained at www.ICGtesting.com
Printed in the USA
BVOW07s1315190215

388263BV00001B/425/P